# Rum 101
## for Dummies Like Me

**JEFF PEDDLE**

RUM 101
*for Dummies Like Me*

Copyright © Jeff Peddle, 2025

All rights reserved. No part of this publication may be reproduced, stored in a retrieval system, or transmitted in any form or by any means, electronic, mechanical, photocopying, recording, or otherwise, without written permission of the author and publisher.

Published by Jeff Peddle, Edmonton, Canada

ISBN:
　　Paperback　　978-1-77354-683-4
　　　　ebook　　978-1-77354-687-2

*All proceeds from this book will go to purchase more rum.*

Publication assistance and digital printing in Canada by

PageMaster.ca

# Contents

INTRODUCTION ..... 1

## Part I - Rum Roots & History ..... 3

### Chapter 1:
What Is Rum, Really? ..... 4

### Chapter 2
Rum and Colonization –
The French, Spanish, and English Influence ..... 6

### Chapter 3
The Dark History – Slavery, Trade, and the Price of Rum ..... 10

### Chapter 4
Oysters and Witness Ships – A Taste of the Past ..... 13

### Chapter 5
Rum, Rations & Nelson's Blood ..... 16

### Chapter 6
Shipwreck Rum – Saint Kitts' Liquid Treasure ..... 20

### Chapter 7
Captain Morgan and the Pirate Legacy ..... 22

## PART II - Rum & Revolution ..... 27

### Chapter 8
Bill McCoy – The Real McCoy of Rum Running ..... 28

### Chapter 9
Rum and Prohibition – The American Thirst ..... 31

### Chapter 10
Newfoundland's Rum Trade
& the Trinity Bay Connection ..... 36

### Chapter 11
Islands Apart, But Not So Different ..... 39

### Chapter 12
From Strawberry Hill to 007 – The Blackwell Rum Story ..... 43

### Chapter 13
Big Black Dick – Rum and Branding in Saint Martin ..... 45

### Chapter 14
Rum Roads & Wrong Turns in Anguilla ..... 49

**Chapter 15**
Sailor Jerry and Tattoos at Sea .................................................. 51

**Chapter 16**
Bacardi – Bats, Revolution, and a Family Legacy .................. 55

**Chapter 17**
Lamb's Rum and Newfoundland Pride ................................... 58

**Chapter 18**
The Smuggler's Spirit – Kirk and Sweeney Rum .................... 61

**Chapter 19**
The Prince to Peddler Program –
COVID, Curried Goat, and Chairman's Reserve .................... 64

**Chapter 20**
Brazil's Cachaça vs. Rum – Juice or Molasses? ....................... 67

**Chapter 21**
Haitian Rum — Resilience in a Bottle .................................... 70

# PART III - Rum Across The Map ........................................ 73

**Chapter 22**
The Rocky Mountain Rum-Runners –
Crowsnest Pass and the Alberta Connection .......................... 74

**Chapter 23**
Romero Distilling –
Rum, Rhymes, and the Spirit of Crowsnest Pass .................... 77

**Chapter 24**
"Brum" with a View –
A Toast to Rig Hand and a Good Buddy ................................ 80

**Chapter 25**
U.S. Military in Newfoundland –
Coca-Cola, Rum, and Culture Clash ....................................... 83

**Chapter 26**
Al Capone and Rum in St. Pierre & Miquelon ....................... 86

**Chapter 27**
From Plantation to Planteray .................................................. 91

**Chapter 28**
My Trip to Barbados –
St. Nicholas Abbey, Rum as Religion
& West Indies Distillery ........................................................... 94

**Chapter 29**
Dominican Republic –
Ron, Roots, and a Touch of Mamajuana Magic ................... 104

**Chapter 30**
My Trip to China –
Bathroom Shocks and the Search for Rum .......................... 108

**Chapter 31**
The Philippines' Liquid Legend –
Tanduay & Tondena Rum ..................................................111

**Chapter 32**
India – Rum, Spice, and Unexpected Adventures ................113

**Chapter 33**
Thailand –
Rum, Rice, and the Tropical Twist You Didn't See Coming...117

**Chapter 34**
Gosling's Rum: The Grand Plan Gone Wrong ..................... 120

**Chapter 35**
From Icebergs to Iguanas:
How the Rock Powered Belize ............................................ 122

**Chapter 36**
The Rum Raid of 1926 – Belize's Bold Rebellion ................ 125

**Chapter 37**
Rum and Uncle Sam –
How the U.S. Government Got Into Booze ........................ 127

**Chapter 38**
A Shot of Rum with Your Cough Syrup,
Prescriptions & Prohibition ................................................ 130

**Chapter 39**
Rum in the White House –
President Harding's Wet Cabinet.........................................131

**Chapter 40**
NASCAR & Rumrunners –
From Booze to Burnouts ....................................................133

**Chapter 41**
Spirits, Superstitions & the Rum That Sees All ...................135

**Chapter 42**
The West Indies Rum Syndicate – Caribbean Cartels .........137

**Chapter 43**
Bathtub Rum – America's Homebrew Havoc......................139

**Chapter 44**
Rum Running by Sea Plane –
Sky Smugglers of Prohibition..............................................141

**Chapter 45**
Rum Runners' Row – New Jersey's Boozy Shoreline...........143

**Chapter 46**
The French Foreign Legion and Liquid Courage .................145

**Chapter 47**
Fake Lighthouses and Florida Keys' Rum Havens ...............147

### Chapter 48
Puerto Rico's Sugar Wars and Tax Rebellions ....................149

### Chapter 49
Puerto Rican Rums:
The Powerhouse of the Caribbean… Without a Vote ...........151

### Chapter 50
Harlem Renaissance and Rum's Jazz Legacy ......................153

### Chapter 51
I Drink Rum to Save the Planet (You're Welcome)...............155

## PART IV - Newfoundland's Rum Legacy ............................. 159

### Chapter 52
The Rums of Newfoundland – Heritage in Every Bottle....... 160

### Chapter 53
Made on the Rock –
The Rums of Newfoundland & the Screech-In Tradition ..... 164

### Chapter 54
Newfoundland Distillery in Clarke Beach ............................173

## Part V - Bonus Bar .................................................................. 179

Top Rums to Try Before You Die .......................................... 180

My Personal Collection & Rare Finds ...................................183

Rum and Food Pairings.........................................................189

Sources & Acknowledgments ................................................ 194

Final Toast – "May Yer Big Jib Always Draw" ...................... 196

About the Author .................................................................. 198

# INTRODUCTION

Rum isn't just a drink—it's a story in a bottle. A wild, wandering, wave-crashing, cannon-blasting, belly-laughing, sometimes tear-jerking story. And this book? Well, this is my way of pouring out that story one glass at a time—just for dummies like me who didn't realize there was so much history, heartbreak, and hilarity behind one little bottle of booze.

I was born in Labrador City in 1967, but it was Newfoundland that shaped me. I spent years working on George Street—the kind of place where stories are born, rum is poured, and the occasional bouncer (yes, that was me) ends up in a Black Horse beer commercial. Back then, I thought very little about what was in the bottle—only how strong it was, how good it burned, and whether it went well with Coke or Ginger Ale.

Fast forward a few decades, and I found myself neck-deep in rum history, taking the Master Rummelier course under the legendary Greg Hill and Matt Pietrek—two fellas who somehow managed to make molasses sexy. What started as curiosity quickly turned into obsession. I dug into the dark days of slavery, the birth of the Royal Navy's "Nelson's Blood," and how pirates, Prohibition, and even NASCAR all came rum-running into history.

Along the way, I also realized my own family's connection to this incredible journey. My grandfather and father grew up in Heart's Content, Trinity Bay, Newfoundland, where salt cod was loaded up from and brought all the way to Jamaica in the Caribbean. This trade route wasn't just about fish and rum—it was about survival, grit, and the unspoken bond between two very different worlds tied together by barrels and schooners. Under influence Some of my most elegant bottles came not from big distillery tours or flashy bottles, but from quiet shops on the front side of Saint Martin, where I used to walk the streets daily to find a special bottle after four different trips there I had a great grasp of the history and the culture.

So this book? It's part history, part travel diary, part Newfoundland nonsense—and 100% soaked in rum. We'll explore how different empires influenced the style of rum across the Caribbean, how Al Capone stashed it in St. Pierre, and why a bottle of "Big Black Dick" rum might stop a tourist in their tracks. I'll share my visits to distilleries in Barbados, Saint Martin, Thailand, China—and yes, I'll even tell you about that time I squatted in a Chinese toilet and nearly passed out from the smell.

This isn't your average rum book. This one comes with jokes, true stories, Newfie humour, and a warning:

The more you read, the more rum you'll want—and the smarter you'll sound at the bar.

So pour a glass.

Welcome to Rum 101 for Dummies Like Me.

Let's get into it.

# Part I

# Rum Roots & History

## CHAPTER 1:

# What Is Rum, Really?

Rum. The word alone stirs something in the great memories of warm beaches, pirate tales, and that first glorious sip that burns just right. But before we set sail into the rich history, legends, and global impact of rum, let's answer the most basic question:

## What the hell is it, anyway?

At its core, rum is a distilled spirit made from sugarcane—either from molasses (a thick byproduct of refining sugar) or fresh sugarcane juice, like they do in Brazil and parts of the French Caribbean. That's it. But what happens after all that is what makes rum so wild, diverse, and misunderstood.

Before we go too far, though, let's talk about the name itself. The enslaved Africans, who were forced to work the plantations, once called the early, fiery spirit "kill-devil"—because it was so harsh it could chase away demons. Others called it "rumbullion," a slang term meaning uproar or a brawl, which matched the feeling you got after drinking it. Over time, the name was shortened simply to rum. So even the name carries a legacy of pain, survival, and transformation.

## The Basic Recipe:

- Ferment it. (Sugar gets turned into alcohol by yeast.)
- Distill it. (Concentrate the alcohol and flavours.)

- Age it. (Usually in barrels—sometimes new, sometimes used, sometimes charred.)
- Bottle it. (And hopefully drink it responsibly… or with friends.)

## So Why Is There So Much Variety?

Because rum doesn't follow one strict global rulebook like whisky or cognac. It's like the rebel cousin at the family reunion. It can be:

- Light or dark
- Spiced or unflavoured
- Sweet, dry, overproof, or navy strength
- Aged for months or decades
- Distilled in pot stills, column stills, or even old copper kettles from colonial times

Every country and region puts its own spin on rum. The French use fresh cane juice and call it rhum agricole (similar to a from Brazil ). The Spanish often go for smooth, column-distilled aged styles. The English love bold, funky rums packed with molasses and fire. In the Philippines, India, and even Canada, local styles have taken shape.

## So What Makes It Rum?

Here's the short answer:

If it's made from sugarcane, and it makes you smile, it's probably rum.

Some rums are refined, elegant, and worth hundreds of dollars. Others are cheap, cheerful, and best served in a plastic cup on a Friday night. And that's the beauty of it—there's no wrong way to rum. I have visited distilleries all over the world and now and finally now I have a handle on it.

> **If life gives you limes…**
> **Add rum and call it a good day.**

CHAPTER 2

# Rum and Colonization – The French, Spanish, and English Influence

If you want to understand why rum tastes different depending on where it's from, forget the bottles for a minute. Look at the flags.

That's right—whether it was the French, Spanish, or English who colonized a region, their influence determined everything from how rum was made to how it was taxed, traded, and even respected. While I was visiting St. Marten, I came across my first French Rum called JM Rhum Agricole.

## The English: Bold, Funky, and Full of Fire

The British didn't invent rum, but they did turn it into a global industry. Think of places like Jamaica, Barbados, Guyana—these were strongholds of British rum production. They used molasses, relied on pot stills, and embraced long barrel aging. The result? If they conquered it, they made rum there.

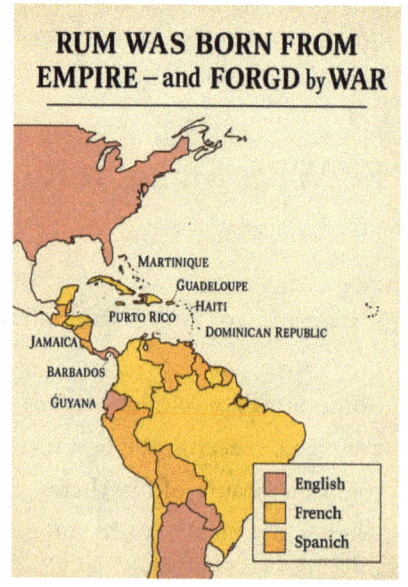

Bold, heavy, funky rums—what rum nerds call "high-ester" rums, loaded with fruity, funky aromas and deep flavour.

And let's not forget the Royal Navy, which made rum a daily ration for sailors for over 300 years. We'll get to that in another Chapter, but spoiler alert: It wasn't for hydration.

## The Spanish: Smooth, Soft, and Silky

In places like Cuba, Puerto Rico, Panama, Colombia, and the Dominican Republic, the Spanish preferred things a bit more… elegant. These rums are usually column distilled, aged in American oak barrels, and filtered for smoothness.

Think of brands like Bacardi, Ron Diplomático, or Don Q—clean, slightly sweet, and made to go down easy.

Spanish-style rum often focuses on balance and accessibility. It's the kind of rum you mix into a perfect mojito or enjoy neat, without lighting your throat on fire.

## The French: Grassy, Green, and Pure Cane Juice

French colonies, like Martinique, Guadeloupe, Réunion Island, and parts of Haiti, went a completely different route. Instead of molasses, they used fresh-pressed sugarcane juice, creating what's known as rhum agricole.

This stuff is sharp, herbal, and intensely flavorful—like sticking your nose into a sugarcane field and taking a shot of sunshine. The French even created the AOC (Appellation d'Origine Contrôlée) system, like in wine, to regulate how it's made in Martinique.

It's artisanal. It's bold. It's the Pinot Noir of the rum world. When I visited Saint Martin, here is where I found my first amazing French rum called Rhum J.M (Martinique).

# French Rums from Saint-Martin – A Taste of the Islands with Parisian Class

Some of my most elegant bottles came not from big distillery tours or flashy bars—but from quiet shops on the French side of Saint-Martin, where the rum is as refined as the accent. This shelf features a few of my favourites from Martinique and Guadeloupe, where they make rhum agricole—rum distilled directly from fresh sugarcane juice, not molasses.

Bottles like Clément VSOP, Saint James Quintessence, and Longueteau XO are more than just rum—they're craftsmanship in a glass. Each one carries the deep earthiness of sugarcane fields, the tropical terroir of the French Caribbean, and the kind of complexity that makes you stop mid-sip and say, "Oh wow."

These rums are often aged in French oak and labelled under strict AOC regulations (Appellation d'Origine Contrôlée), meaning they follow similar rules to French wine. And yes, they're that good.

Most of these bottles came home with me in a suitcase that probably should've had its own boarding pass. But I couldn't leave without them because they don't just taste like rum, they taste like the story of the island. Fun fact; I always declared all my rum coming through customs and very honest. I had no problem paying taxes and never questioned.

# Colonization Didn't Just Shape Rum—It Shaped People

Of course, the spread of rum wasn't just about flavour. It was built on slavery, trade, and warfare. Colonizers didn't just bring distillation techniques—they brought oppression. Entire regions were forced into rum production to fuel the economies of European empires.

The legacy is complicated. But one thing's for sure: The colonial powers may have started it, but the people of these islands perfected it.

Today, the rum world reflects a beautiful mix of rebellion, resilience, and regional pride. Whether you prefer a funky Jamaican, a smooth Cuban, or a grassy agricole—what's in your glass tells the story of empires, revolutions, and survival. We will get into that in later Chapters.

> I tried to mix rum with holy water…
> Now I've got spirits in every sense of the word.

CHAPTER 3

# The Dark History – Slavery, Trade, and the Price of Rum

## For all the sweetness in a bottle of rum, its past is bitter.

Behind every golden pour, behind the cheers and cocktails, there's a legacy of human suffering—a brutal Chapter of history where people were bought, sold, and enslaved to feed the world's insatiable thirst for sugar and spirits.

This is the real cost of rum, and we can't sip honestly without acknowledging it.

## The Triangular Trade

From the 1600s to the 1800s, European powers created a global network of trade that would become known as the Triangular Trade:

1. Europe sent guns, cloth, slave beads and goods to Africa.

Africa sent enslaved people to the Caribbean and Americas. More in Chapters to come on what they ate before their voyage.

2. The Caribbean sent sugar, molasses, and rum back to Europe—and North America.

It was efficient. It was profitable.

And it was built on the backs of millions.

Over 12 million Africans were taken from their homelands—packed onto slave ships like cargo. Witness ships, as some called them, carried men, women, and children across the Middle Passage. Many died along the way. Those who survived were sold to work on sugarcane plantations, particularly in Barbados, Jamaica, Haiti, Martinique, Brazil, and the southern United States.

They worked long, brutal hours. Cane fields were hellish. Distilleries were worse—hot, smoky, and dangerous. Enslaved Africans didn't just harvest the cane… they built the rum industry. All slaves and ships were insured by companies in England. If a ship was going to go down, then all of the slaves go down with it and got the insurance money. It wasn't until one judge ruled against the insurance company. His daughter-in-law happened to be a young coloured woman.

## People for Rum

In some places, people were literally traded for rum.

- A strong male: 160 gallons
- A female: 120 gallons
- A child: 30–40 gallons
- An infant: sometimes considered "optional"

It's sickening. But it happened. And it's part of rum's story.

## The Legacy

Even after slavery was abolished in many places by the mid-1800s, exploitation continued. Indentured labourers from India and China replaced slaves in some colonies. Many distilleries stayed profitable through systemic oppression and poverty. One of the distilleries I visited in Barbados still has the most beautiful home and chandeliers made from seashells.

But over time, the descendants of those who suffered became the keepers of the culture—the rum makers, blenders, and storytellers who turned pain into pride. Today, many of the finest rums in the world come from countries where rum once symbolized chains—and now symbolizes freedom, art, and identity.

This Chapter is not here to bring you down.

It's here to raise awareness.

If we're going to raise a glass, let's also raise the truth. Because knowing the history makes every sip more meaningful.

> I once asked a fella if he preferred dark or light rum. He said, 'Depends if the power's out.'

CHAPTER 4

# Oysters and Witness Ships – A Taste of the Past

Today, oysters are served on crushed ice with champagne. They're delicacies, luxuries—slurped at high-end restaurants by people in tailored suits. But once, oysters were the last meal of the enslaved—and they tell a powerful story. The first time I saw this, I watched it on a show with Morgan Freeman, and then I took a dive and did a lot of research that left me absolutely shocked. Some men carried tusks and heavy items just to get to the ship.

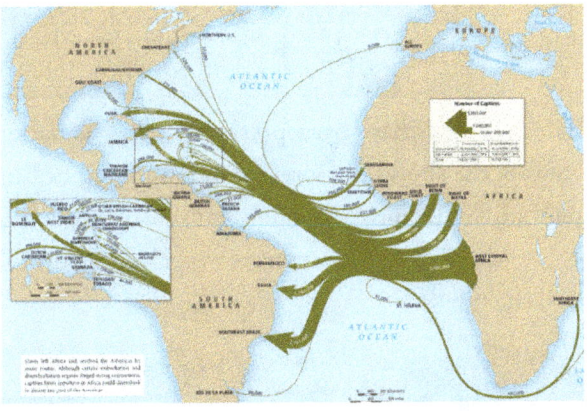

Before enslaved Africans were forced aboard the dreaded witness ships—those vessels that carried human lives across the Atlantic—they were kept in holding areas near the coast of West Africa. These places were grim, often referred to as slave castles or forts, with dark dungeons that smelled of fear and death. When I was in Barbados, I witnessed photos and slave ships and how they were built.

Outside, these forts, by the water, were miles and miles of oyster shells—piled high like hills. Not because of celebration or feasts, but because

13

oysters were the only food the enslaved were given before being loaded onto ships. Easy to harvest, high in protein, and free.

They were fed just enough to survive the horrific journey known as the Middle Passage, where many would die, chained together in their own filth, stacked like lumber. The ships that carried them? Coldly referred to as witness ships—because they witnessed humanity at its worst.

Many of these coastlines have been preserved today as national historic parks. If you walk the shores of Goree Island (Senegal) or Elmina Castle (Ghana), you'll still find remnants—mountains of oyster shells—marking the final meals of those whose names were never written down, but whose stories echo in the tide.

**A SACRED BAOBAB STANDS OVER MOUNDS OF OYSTER SHELLS — A SILENT WITNESS TO THE CENTURIES-OLD SLAVE TRADE ALONG AFRICA'S COAST.**

## Rum's Role

These ships didn't just carry people—they carried molasses and rum back to Europe and the Americas. Every drop of rum from that era was soaked in sorrow. It's why modern distillers and rum historians insist we tell the full story—not to guilt the present, but to honour the past. Because all of the rum was going back-and-forth, to which we will get into in later Chapters, but Pirates were on the rise.

So next time someone offers you oysters with a glass of rum in a fancy bar or by the ocean pause for a moment. Not just to savour the flavour—but to remember the people who never had a choice and those shorelines in Africa.

"Mountains of oyster shells line the path to the coast — haunting reminders of the meager food once given to enslaved Africans before their forced voyage across the Atlantic

> Rum in the Caribbean is like oxygen—if you're not using it, you're probably not alive.

CHAPTER 5

# Rum, Rations & Nelson's Blood

"Join the army," they said. "See the world," they said. They forgot to mention the rum—and that's where things got interesting.

When I was just sixteen or seventeen, I signed up with the 56 Field Engineer Squadron in St. John's, Newfoundland. It was a proud moment—and a turning point in my life. I had the honour of training at Gagetown, New Brunswick, and later, helping build a suspension bridge across Wallace Brook in Gros Morne National Park. We weren't just building bridges—we were building memories (and sneaking in the odd drink of beer and rum when no one was looking).

That was when my fascination with rum really kicked off.

One of the first names I came across in my rum journey was Lemon Hart and Son—a name forever tied to British naval tradition. Founded in 1804, Lemon Hart became the official rum supplier to the British Royal Navy, and their dark Guyanese rum was handed out as daily rations to sailors around the world.

But how did rum become such a naval staple?

Enter Vice Admiral Edward Vernon—a man remembered just as much for his clothing as for his commands. He wore a distinctive grogram coat, a coarse, ribbed fabric made of silk and wool. His sailors affectionately (or not-so-affectionately) called him "Old Grog."

In 1740, Vernon issued an order to cut the sailors' rum with water to reduce drunkenness and maintain order at sea. That watered-down rum quickly became known as "grog", named after the man in the grogram coat.

And just like that, rum history was made—by a jacket!

Of course, sailors weren't always thrilled. Some added lime or sugar to the mix, giving rise to early rum punches and even helping prevent scurvy. From there, the daily "tot" became sacred tradition, and Lemon Hart flowed freely across decks from the Caribbean to the English Channel.

## Black Tot: The Last Drop of Empire

Imagine sipping a piece of naval history — not just a rum, but the final remnants of a centuries-old tradition that once fuelled the might of the British Empire. That's exactly what you get with Black Tot: Last Consignment — a rum that isn't just rare, it's irreplaceable.

On July 31, 1970, known forever as Black Tot Day, the Royal Navy ended its daily rum ration after 300 years. The sailors protested, held mock funerals, and poured their final tots with heavy hearts. But the Navy didn't dump the remaining barrels — they sealed them in flagons and tucked them away in bonded warehouses.

Decades later, just 5,000 bottles were drawn from those very flagons — untouched since the '70s — and bottled as Black Tot: Last Consignment. Containing rums aged from Jamaica, Trinidad, and Guyana, some over 40 years old, it's a rich, brooding, oak-heavy blend of colonial era strength and seafaring tradition. The box alone looks like it belongs in a museum — and honestly, it should.

This isn't rum for cocktails — this is rum for reflection. Every sip carries echoes of Admiral Rodney's battles, Caribbean trade winds, and Royal

Navy tradition. It's a rum so rare that collectors guard it like gold and enthusiasts whisper about it like legend.

And just like Ragged Rock Rum from Newfoundland, which pays tribute to its rugged heritage and local spirit, Black Tot is more than just a label. It's a liquid time capsule, a drink that tells a story — and maybe a warning — about the end of an era. I am honoured to have two bottles in my personal collection worth $1600.00 per bottle. The last place to stop giving rum rations was Canada in 1970.

My own rum collection now holds some real naval treasures, including:

- Admiral Rodney Rum, honouring the 1782 Battle of the Saintes.
- Pusser's Rum, based on the Royal Navy's original recipe.
- Pusser's Rum, Gunpowder Proof
- Black Tot Rum, bottled from the very last Navy rations served in 1970.
- Inspired by tradition, unhindered by convention. This is a rich, golden marriage of fruity Barbadian, full-bodied Guyanese and vibrant Jamaican rums that warms the soul. Sip it or mix it, you'll never forget it."
- London Dock Rum, bold and spiced like the shipyards themselves.
- And, of course, Nelson's Blood.

Now here's a tale for the ages: When Admiral Horatio Nelson died at sea during the Battle of Trafalgar, his crew—determined to fulfill his dying wish—placed his body in a barrel of rum to preserve it for the journey back to England.

But sailors will be sailors.

They drilled holes in the barrel, inserted straws, and took sips of the rum as they sailed home. By the time they arrived, the rum was gone, and Nelson had been well and truly marinated. That preserved spirit came to be known as "Nelson's Blood."

*Images: Lemon Hart and Son: Official purveyor of Royal Navy rum, and a true legend in my collection. Every drop carries over 200 years of naval history.*

"We never called it grog—we just called it breakfast

CHAPTER 6

# Shipwreck Rum – Saint Kitts' Liquid Treasure

In the serene Caribbean jewel of Saint Kitts and Nevis, rum is more than a drink—it's a liquid chronicle of the island's rich naval past. Few brands embody this maritime legacy more vividly than Shipwreck Rum, whose very name evokes images of sunken treasure, cannon fire, and the roaring age of sail.

The tale behind Shipwreck Rum begins in 1782, during the Battle of the Saintes—a fierce naval clash between Britain and France that helped decide the fate of the Caribbean. Among the British fleet was the **Admiral Rodney**, a celebrated Royal Navy commander whose tactical genius secured a decisive victory. But history didn't sail away untouched—one of the British troopships, believed to be part of Rodney's fleet, met its end off the coast of Saint Kitts. Onboard were soldiers, supplies, and most famously—barrels of rum. Some of that cargo was salvaged by locals, and legend has it that the rum was so good, it sparked both stories and spirits for generations to come.

Fast forward to today, and the Brinley Gold Shipwreck Rum brand keeps that story alive. Crafted on the island of Saint Kitts, each bottle is a tribute to that fateful wreck. Their small-batch rums—like Vanilla, Coconut, Mango, and Spiced Rum—are handcrafted using pure island cane and real ingredients, delivering rich Caribbean flavor with every sip.

Though Saint Kitts doesn't boast a multitude of distilleries, what it does offer is depth—of character, history, and authenticity. Shipwreck Rum is more than a beverage; it's a vessel of the island's colonial heritage, seafaring pride, and tropical allure.

Whether you sip it neat, in a breezy beachside cocktail, or over ice as the sun dips below the horizon, Shipwreck Rum is a salute to the sea—a tribute to Admiral Rodney's legacy, a stormy night in 1782, and the golden spirit that washed ashore.

I was told to drink responsibly, so I never spill a drop.

CHAPTER 7

# Captain Morgan and the Pirate Legacy

When Captain Morgan rum hit the market, its target demographic was primarily young adult males, especially in the 18–34 age range (legal drinking age depending on country), with a focus on those who enjoyed casual social drinking and parties. But most don't know he was an actual privateer. Let me tell you the story and pick back up here at the end with a seagrams company in Canada.

Before he became the smiling face behind one of the most recognizable rum bottles in the world, Captain Henry Morgan was something very real: a privateer, pirate, and post-war politician who helped carve the Caribbean into the image of colonial conquest—and left his mark on rum history forever. But most don't know he was an actual privateer.

## From Wales to the West Indies

Henry Morgan was born in Wales around 1635. Like many young men of his time, he left for the New World as a soldier of fortune. But in the Caribbean, he didn't just fight battles—he wrote the playbook for pirate warfare.

With the blessing of the British Crown, Morgan became a privateer,

meaning he had legal permission to rob, plunder, and burn anything belonging to the Spanish. In 1671, he led a legendary assault on Panama City, marching his men through the jungle, defeating the Spanish, and leaving the city in smouldering ruins.

His actions were so bold, even Britain had to pretend to be shocked. He was arrested and sent to London… where he was promptly knighted and made Lieutenant Governor of Jamaica. You couldn't make this up.

## Conquest Never Really Stopped

Here's what I found on the places he did invade:

1. Porto Bello (Panama) – 1668
   A heavily fortified Spanish port. Morgan and his men stormed it, tortured locals, and made off with thousands in treasure.
2. Maracaibo (Venezuela) – 1669
   He raided the town, fought off three Spanish ships in a daring escape, and sailed off rich.
3. Panama City (Panama) – 1671
   His biggest haul and most famous raid—done after peace was declared. The city was burned to the ground.
4. Puerto Principe (Cuba) – Early in his career
   Another town sacked for rum, silver, and all things shiny.

Morgan was part of a broader trend—the age of profit by-conquest, where nations used men like him to continue expanding, even during peacetime. His raids weren't rogue missions; they were extensions of empire-building.

The Caribbean was a chessboard, and rum, sugar, and slavery were the pawns. Morgan knew it—and played the game well.

## Rum, Retirement, and a Watery Grave

Despite his bloodstained résumé, Morgan settled into a strange kind of respectability. He drank heavily, enforced rum laws in Jamaica, and died in 1688 in Port Royal—then called the "wickedest city on Earth."

Captain Henry Morgan didn't go out with a whimper—he had a full state funeral in 1688 in Port Royal, Jamaica, the most notorious pirate city in the world at the time.

Here's what we know about his funeral:

- A State Funeral Fit for a legendary pirate, national hero, and feared by many.
- Morgan died on August 25, 1688, likely from complications related to alcohol, tuberculosis, or the lingering effects of tropical diseases and old battle wounds.
- Despite his piratical past, he was honoured as a national hero by the English colonial government.

After a tsunami in 1692, much of Port Royal, including Morgan's tomb, was swallowed by the sea. Some say his spirit still haunts the rum cellars beneath the waves.

## From Blood to Branding

In 1944, long after Morgan's bones had been lost to the sea, the Seagram Company in Canada saw potential in the legend. They trademarked Captain Morgan and launched a sweet, spiced rum that would become a global juggernaut.

Today, the Captain is more likely to show up at a football tailgate than a cannonball raid—but the spirit of conquest lives on in his name, label, and laugh.

So next time you sip Captain Morgan, remember:

You're not just drinking a party rum.

You're tasting a legacy of wars, invasions, and one man who kept fighting long after the flags were folded—and is now bottled, branded, and still raising hell on liquor shelves around the world. Cheers, Captain.

> Captain Morgan doesn't need a compass.
> Wherever he stands becomes the centre of the party.

# Pirate Superstitions

*From the Seven Seas and Beyond – Where Rum and Lore Collide*

**1. Whistling on a Ship**
Bad luck! Whistling was believed to "whistle up a storm." Sailors thought it tempted the wind gods to unleash their fury.

**2. The Albatross**
Considered a sacred bird. Killing one was sure to bring misfortune. It was said to carry the souls of dead sailors.

**3. Bananas on Board**
No bananas on a ship! This superstition came from bad voyages where food spoiled, ships disappeared, or fish weren't biting—all blamed on bananas.

**4. Red Sky at Night / Red Sky in Morning**
"Red sky at night, sailor's delight. Red sky in morning, sailor's warning."
A red sunrise was thought to signal storms or bloodshed at sea. ( still used the Newfoundland daily.)

**5. Women on Board**
Many pirates believed women brought bad luck aboard a ship. Ironically, some of the fiercest pirates were women—Anne Bonny and Mary Read would disagree. ( judges are still out on this one.)

**6. The Left Foot First**
Starting any journey by stepping with your left foot was considered bad luck—especially boarding a ship.

**7. Tattoos & Earrings**
Sailors wore gold earrings not just for fashion, but as insurance—to pay for a proper burial. Tattoos of anchors or swallows were seen as good luck charms.

**8. Touching Wood**
The origin of "knock on wood." Sailors would touch the wooden parts of a ship for protection against misfortune.

**9. No Farewells at the Dock**
Saying goodbye before a voyage was avoided—it was thought to tempt fate.

**10. The Flying Dutchman**
A ghost ship doomed to sail forever. To see it meant doom. Many sailors swore they saw her on stormy nights after a bit too much rum…but of course years later, they named a rum after it, I have in my collection

# PART II

# Rum & Revolution

CHAPTER 8

# Bill McCoy – The Real McCoy of Rum Running

When Prohibition gripped the United States in the 1920s, bootleggers became outlaws, and outlaws became legends. But Bill McCoy wasn't your average crook. He didn't water down his product. He didn't bribe politicians. And he didn't cross into U.S. waters.

He just outsmarted everyone.

That's why, to this day, when people say something is "the real McCoy," they're tipping their hat to a rum runner with a moral compass and a damn good business plan.

## From Yacht Builder, to Outlaw Entrepreneur

Bill McCoy started as a respected yacht builder in Florida with his brother Ben. Bill and his brother Ben were standing in front of the ship building shop out of work. Until, a friend drove up in a fancy car and suit, and told them both about his new entrepreneurial way of bringing rum from the Caribbean into the US.

But when Prohibition hit in 1920, the boat business dried up—and liquor became the new currency.

So McCoy did what any clever capitalist might do:

He bought a ship, filled it with the finest Caribbean rum he could find, and parked it just outside U.S. waters—three miles offshore.

He never broke the law. He let smaller boats come to him, load up, and return to shore. It was brilliant. No bribes. No poison booze. Just pure product and international loopholes.

## Rum Row and the Floating Liquor Store

McCoy's ship, the Tomoka, became a fixture on Rum Row—a string of vessels anchored off the East Coast selling spirits to anyone with a boat and guts. He stocked it with Barbados rum, Cuban aguardiente, and British gin. Everything was top-shelf.

People trusted McCoy's booze because it wasn't cut, spiked, or faked. It was the real thing—hence, "the Real McCoy."

He even used clever branding:

Some bottles had wax seals, others had secret marks. At one point, he even sold rum in coconut shells, so it looked like tropical souvenirs instead of contraband.

## The Chase for the Real McCoy

The U.S. Coast Guard Cutter Seneca was given a clear mission: capture Bill McCoy, the most notorious and "honest" rum-runner of the Prohibition era, even if it meant doing so in international waters.

A dramatic sea chase unfolded, with Seneca closing in fast. As shells exploded across the bow of his vessel, McCoy had no choice but to surrender. The legend had been cornered.

## Justice for the Gentleman Smuggler

McCoy was sentenced to nine months in prison, and true to his word as a principled outlaw, he served his time without complaint. Remarkably, he never returned to rum-running—leaving behind a legacy of high-seas smuggling, clean-cut ethics, and one unforgettable name: The Real McCoy.

## Legacy in a Bottle

Today, McCoy's story lives on—not just in sayings, but in rum brands that carry his name. His approach was honest, smart, and ahead of its time.

He proved that even in the darkest days of bootlegging, you could still have standards.

So here's to Bill McCoy—

The only smuggler who broke the law without ever breaking his word.

> I asked the bartender for something strong.
> He handed me a mirror and said, "Face your problems."

CHAPTER 9

# Rum and Prohibition – The American Thirst

## First of All, Who Started Prohibition and Why?

Prohibition in the United States wasn't started by one single group—it was the result of a powerful alliance of three major movements, each with its own motivations but a common goal: to ban alcohol.

### 1. The Temperance Movement

- Led by groups like the Women's Christian Temperance Union (WCTU) and The Anti-Saloon League.
- Believed alcohol was the root of domestic abuse, poverty, and moral decline.
- Strongly backed by Christian values and seen as a way to protect families and women from the consequences of drunkenness.

### 2. Religious and Moral Reformers

- Evangelical Protestants, Baptists, and Methodists were heavily involved.
- Saw alcohol as sinful and pushed for a "dry" America based on religious convictions.
- Sunday sermons often became anti-alcohol platforms.

### 3. Political and Business Interests

- Industrialists and factory owners, like Henry Ford, wanted sober, efficient workers.
- Believed banning alcohol would increase productivity and reduce workplace accidents.
- Politicians jumped on the movement to gain support from church groups and social reformers.

## Prohibition Fueled Hate: How the KKK Rose Under

The KKK used this chaos and probation as an opportunity to position themselves as "moral enforcers" of Prohibition laws, gaining support by attacking immigrants, Catholics, Jews, and Black Americans—groups they blamed for the rise in alcohol consumption. They portrayed themselves as defenders of American values and law and order, recruiting millions of members during the 1920s. In reality, they used the Prohibition era as a cover to spread hate, violence, and white supremacy under the guise of patriotism and purity.

Together, these three forces created enough pressure to pass the 18th Amendment in 1919 and the Volstead Act to enforce it, ushering in the Prohibition era from 1920 to 1933.

When the U.S. government tried to dry out the country in 1920, they didn't just ban alcohol—they created a national obsession with it. Bars were shut down, distilleries were raided, and liquor became illegal overnight. But Americans didn't stop drinking.

They just got creative—and very, very thirsty.

Enter: rum.

# Why Rum Took the Lead.

## By boat, train, sled and even sea planes (and we will talk about that later).

Whiskey was harder to get. Beer spoiled quickly. But rum?

It was tropical, abundant, and close—thanks to the Caribbean islands, Canada, and nearby St. Pierre and Miquelon, where liquor was still legal.

Within months, rum was being smuggled into the U.S. by boat, train, sled, and even sea plane (as you saw earlier). The coastlines of Florida, New Jersey, and Newfoundland lit up with activity. Speedboats zipped through the night. Dockworkers got generous bonuses. Politicians turned a blind eye, or better yet, took a cut.

## The Rise of the Speakeasy

With legal bars shut down, secret bars—speakeasies—popped up everywhere. And guess what the drink of choice was?

Rum cocktails.

Bartenders got inventive. They mixed low-quality rum with juices, bitters, spices, and sugar to mask the burn. Many of today's classic cocktails—like the Daiquiri, Rum Punch, and even the early versions of the Mai Tai—evolved during this time.

Some speakeasies had codes to get in. Others were inside barber shops, laundromats, or bakeries. Some had trapdoors, tunnels, and revolving bookcases. All had rum, if you knew who to ask.

## Organized Crime and the Rum Syndicates

While whiskey smuggling was often run by gangsters like Al Capone, rum had its own cast of characters—family crews, ex-sailors, Caribbean traders, and even retired Navy men.

In many ways, rum smuggling was more international, more seaborne, and more rooted in tradition.

Even U.S. Coast Guard officers couldn't keep up. Some were under funded, others were on the take. In one famous quote, a rum runner said:

"For every boat they catch, ten more make it through."

# The End of Prohibition—and Rum's Permanent Seat at the Table

Prohibition was repealed in 1933, and the country breathed a boozy sigh of relief. But the rum didn't fade away. In fact, it had carved out its place. Caribbean producers saw a massive boom. American tastes had shifted.

Rum had gone from a colonial leftover to a mainstream spirit—thanks to speakeasies, smugglers, and one wild decade of thirst.

So when you toast with rum today, you're toasting a time when people weren't just drinking—they were rebelling, surviving, and redefining freedom… one bottle at a time.

> Why did the rum go to therapy?
> It had too many bottled-up emotions.

CHAPTER 10

# Newfoundland's Rum Trade & the Trinity Bay Connection

## The Newfoundland–Jamaica Trade Connection

I grew up in Wabush Labrador, but every summer we'd pack up and travel down to Corner Brook, where my mother was from, and eventually to Heart's Content in Trinity Bay, the town my father called home. Back then, I was just a boy running around the wharves, skipping rocks, and staring at boats I couldn't name—never realizing that years later, I'd be writing stories about those very waters.

It turns out, the quiet coves and outports I visited as a child were once key players in a roaring Atlantic trade. Long before container ships and air freight, a remarkable route connected Newfoundland's rugged coastlines to the warm, tropical harbours of Jamaica. It was a grassroots exchange—built on barrels of salted cod and crates of overproof rum—that tied together two very different worlds across thousands of miles of sea.

At the heart of this connection were Newfoundland's coastal communities: Trinity Bay, Bonavista Bay, Conception Bay, and beyond. From small outports like Heart's Content, Old Perlican, Catalina, and Bonavista, schooners set sail with holds full of cod, timber, and trade goods—destined for the islands of the Caribbean.

# Trinity Bay and Beyond – Newfoundland's Salt Cod Arteries

Communities across Newfoundland's east coast were sustained by the fishery. Throughout the summer, fishermen caught cod, split it, salted it, and laid it out to dry on flakes. This "dried and salted cod" was durable, protein-rich, and ideal for export.

Ports like Grates Cove, Elliston, Trinity, and Carbonear became bustling hubs of activity. Schooners—ranging from 50 to 90 feet in length—were built locally and crewed by tight-knit teams of 5 to 15 men. These vessels would depart in late summer or fall, bound for the warmer waters of the Caribbean.

# A Typical Trade Voyage

- Departure Ports: Trinity Bay, Bonavista Bay, Conception Bay (e.g., Heart's Content, Bonavista, Carbonear)
- Vessel: Two-masted wooden schooners
- Crew Size: 5 to 15 men
- Duration: 3–6 weeks one-way (longer with storms)
- Hazards: Fierce weather, sea sickness, navigation errors, and financial risks

These were no pleasure cruises. Crews faced rough seas, hurricanes, tropical diseases, and the possibility of returning empty-handed if markets soured or goods spoiled.

# Salt Cod for Rum – A Cultural Exchange

In Jamaica, salt cod was in high demand. It became a staple food—especially in ackee and saltfish, now the country's national dish. Cheap, nutritious, and non-perishable, Newfoundland cod helped feed generations of Caribbean families.

In exchange, Newfoundland received:

- Molasses
- Raw cane sugar
- Citrus and spices
- And most famously, high-proof Jamaican rum

Back in Newfoundland, rum became woven into the cultural fabric—poured at weddings, wakes, outport card games, and the kitchen table alike. Strong, sweet, and sometimes deadly potent, it earned its place in both tradition and storytelling.

## The Legacy of the Route

Though the era of rum-running schooners has long passed, its legacy lives on. Newfoundland's kitchen parties still serve up salt fish and strong drink, and the influence of those trade voyages can still be tasted in every bottle of dark rum poured during a family gathering.

The brave mariners who sailed from Trinity Bay, Bonavista Bay, and beyond built more than trade—they built a bridge between worlds. A salty, spirited bond that persists in culture, cuisine and beautiful memories

TRINITY BAY NEWFOUNDLAND, THE VIEW FROM MY PARENTS HOUSE LOOKING OUT THE BAY

> "They say salt cod built Jamaica's belly and rum filled Newfoundland's soul—proof that the best trades are the ones that get everyone fed and half-cut."

CHAPTER 11

# Islands Apart, But Not So Different

## Jamaica & Newfoundland

I've visited Jamaica over a dozen times and fallen in love with the people, the culture, the music, and, of course—the rum. I've toured the Appleton Estate three times, and even made my way to the legendary Monymusk Distillery. But the more I explored, the more something unexpected happened. As different as Jamaica and Newfoundland seem at first glance, when you dig a little deeper, they start to feel like long-lost cousins—separated by geography, maybe, but connected by resilience, storytelling, and a shared love of rum.

In Newfoundland, we had fish and brewis. In Jamaica, it was ackee and salt fish. Both dishes came from the same need: to stretch a salted fish and make it feed a family. It wasn't fancy, but it was survival—and love.

Open any pantry on the Rock, and you'd find Maple Leaf Vienna sausages. In Jamaica? Grace Vienna sausages. Whether you're up in the hills of Portland Parish or out around Bonavista Bay, Vienna sausages were a quick fix when times were tough and mouths were many.

And then there was soup. We made chicken soup to cure the cold, mend a hangover, or feed the crowd on a Sunday. Jamaicans had cock soup—strong, spicy, and full of surprise. I still remember the first time I ordered it and a few "unchopped" chicken parts floated to the top. Let's just say, no pedicure was done before dinner. That chicken had a rough life.

What really connects us, though, isn't just the food—it's the grit. Both places are dotted with small communities where people scrape by, holding tight to tradition. Fishing villages, where boats go out in the morning and hope comes back in the evening. Where a good haul means food on the table, and a bad season means holding your breath 'til next year.

*Jamaican Rum*

Tourism came, but never like the brochures promised. In Jamaica, big resorts sit beside tin-roof homes. In Newfoundland, we painted up a few saltboxes and called it charm—but many communities still rely on EI, side jobs, or heading "out West" to survive. Both islands are filled with proud people who hustle hard and laugh harder.

And when the sun sets? That's when the rum comes out. In Newfoundland, it's Screech or Old Sam. In Jamaica, it's Wray and Nephew or Appleton. Either way, it's served strong, poured generously, and followed by a story, a tune, or maybe a half-drunk debate about who had it harder growing up.

So yeah—different accents, different weather, but the same island heart. We knew struggle. We knew community. And we damn well knew how to make a meal out of nothing and a celebration out of hardship.

The moment you land in Jamaica and hear someone say "Wagwan?"—the local way of saying "What's going on?"—you're not just greeted, you're welcomed. Before long, someone's handing you a glass of roe (that's

Jamaican slang for rum), and reminding you that life is meant to be enjoyed, not endured. Everything just feels… eerie.

To prove how close these islands really are in spirit, just listen to what the locals say:

Jamaican Sayings

- "Wi likkle but wi tallawah."
  (We're small, but we're strong and mighty.)
- "Every mickle mek a muckle."
  (Every little bit adds up to something big.)
- "Walk good."
  (Take care / Safe travels.)

Newfoundland Sayings

- "Stay where you're to, till I comes where you're at."
  (Don't move—I'll come to you.)
- "Long may your big jib draw."
  (May the wind always be in your sails.)
- "Who knit ya?"
  (Who's your people?)

Rum, music, and talking all day—whether it's a reggae beat in Kingston or a kitchen party in Heart's Content, both islands know how to lift a glass and spin a yarn. And if you're lucky enough to experience both, you'll know exactly what I mean.

## Sprats, Caplin, and Silver Bellies – A Backyard Bond Between Islands

On a trip to Jamaica, I found myself off the beaten path, sharing a rum and sorrel on the back patio of a local mason (was it the ring or the handshake, I will leave you guessing) . Like any good islander, he had a little grill fired up and started tossing on these tiny fish, sizzling in oil, seasoned with garlic, Scotch bonnet, and thyme.

I looked down at the silvery little things and nearly choked on my drink.

"Buddy," I said, "you're cooking caplin!"

He laughed. "Caplin? What's that, man?"

# Jamaican Sprats

"You're telling me you've never heard of caplin?" I replied, half in disbelief. "That's what we call these little silver-bellied fish in Newfoundland. They roll in with the tide and we scoop 'em up by the bucket. They're free, they're everywhere, and they're fried on just about every beach from Port aux Basques to St. Anthony."

He squinted at the sprats in the pan. "Nah, man. These sprats are Jamaican. That's island fish."

And that's when it hit me: we were both right.

Newfoundland, Caplin, Two islands, thousands of miles apart, frying up the same little fish, sipping rum, and telling stories. The seasoning was different, the slang was different, but the spirit? The spirit was the same. Whether it's jerk sprats or caplin on the beach, it always goes better with a little rum and good company.

Jamaican version:
Me: "Is this your first glass of rum?"
Him: "Today, yes."
Newfoundland version:
"The only thing stronger than a Newfie's rum pour is his aunt's opinion—and you better agree with both."

CHAPTER 12

# From Strawberry Hill to 007 – The Blackwell Rum Story

The first time I drove up to Strawberry Hill, I felt like I was entering another world — one where time slows down, the mist hugs the mountains, and the rum tastes just a little better because of the view.

The winding road from Kingston twisted and climbed like a snake through the Blue Mountains, and with every turn, the city shrank below. When I finally reached the top, the view took my breath away. You could see Kingston Harbour off in the distance, as if you were floating above the island itself.

The air was cooler up there — crisp and sweet, scented with tropical flowers and a hint of woodsmoke. I wandered the grounds past gingerbread cottages and hammocks swaying gently in the breeze. Then I saw it — the infinity pool, perched on the edge of the hill like it had been poured straight from heaven. I sat beside it with a cocktail in hand, the glass sweating, the ice clinking softly, and I thought, "This might just be the most peaceful spot in Jamaica."

But Strawberry Hill isn't just a resort — it's a piece of history. This estate was once a refuge for artists, mystics, and musicians. And the man behind it all? Chris Blackwell, the founder of Island Records and the producer who gave the world Bob Marley, Grace Jones, U2, and many more. Blackwell grew up in Jamaica, and after conquering the music world, he came home to honor his roots.

That's how Blackwell Rum was born — a deep, rich "Black Gold" Jamaican rum crafted in tribute to the island that shaped him. The label even features a map of Jamaica with places that meant something to him: Goldeneye (his home on the north coast and the birthplace of James Bond), Strawberry Hill, and more. Every bottle tells part of his story — and Jamaica's.

And if that wasn't cool enough, he added a secret agent twist. Chris Blackwell was a producer on several James Bond films, and to celebrate the 60th anniversary of 007, he released the Blackwell 007 Limited Edition — a matte black bottle with a golden Bond logo, as smooth and bold as the spy himself.

So there I was, high in the Blue Mountains, sipping Blackwell rum by the pool, with reggae playing softly in the distance and mist curling through the palms. In that moment, I realized that rum isn't just a drink here — it's a lifestyle, a soundtrack, and a passport to Jamaican culture.

From Strawberry Hill to Kingston, from music studios to Bond sets, Blackwell's story — and his rum — captures it all

*View from Strawberry Hill Resort infinity pool*

**In the Caribbean, they don't call it a drinking problem—they call it local culture.**

CHAPTER 13

# Big Black Dick – Rum and Branding in Saint Martin

Of all the rum names in the world, none gets more raised eyebrows, cheeky grins, and souvenir sales than Big Black Dick. Yes, that's a real rum—and yes, there's a wild story behind it.

This isn't just marketing. It's myth, mischief, and money-making genius, all wrapped in a label guaranteed to make tourists laugh (and reach for their wallets).

## The Legend Behind the Name

According to local lore—blending truth, fiction, and clever storytelling—Big Black Dick was once a West African man named Richard Le Noir, taken from his homeland and enslaved in the Caribbean during the 1700s.

After earning his freedom (some stories say by escaping, others say by working his way out), Richard became a pirate. He was said to have sailed under the British flag, plundered the Spanish Main, and eventually retired to the Cayman Islands, where he used his knowledge of sugarcane to craft his own rum.

Whether or not this version of events is historically accurate, it doesn't matter much—because the story stuck. And in the world of rum, a good legend is worth more than gold doubloons.

## The Rum (and the Ruckus)

Big Black Dick rum is sweet, rich, and Caribbean through and through. It comes in flavours like original dark, vanilla, and coconut, and is often sold in tacky tourist bottles with a pirate label and slogans that toe the line between fun and scandal. They sell it at the waterfront for $40 a bottle

But the real genius? The marketing.

In tourist markets across Saint Martin, I heard local bartenders and vendors say "You ladies want some Big Black Dick?"

It's impossible not to stop—and that's the point.

It gets people laughing, talking, and buying. One bottle becomes a bar conversation for years. They sell it under the waterfront for $40 a bottle.

## Rum, Race, and Reclamation

Now, let's be real: this brand walks a fine line. Some see it as problematic. Others see it as empowerment—a Black man turned legend, reclaiming the pirate fantasy and turning pain into pride (and profit).

And when I walked into a liquor store and saw a bottle for $18, I bought it on the spot.

Later, I auctioned one off at a local rum event in Fort McMurray for $380.

That's right—from the shelf to the stage, Big Black Dick knows how to make an entrance.

## Toppers Rhum – Saint Martin's Colourful Surprise

Visiting Toppers Rhum in Saint Martin was like walking into a rainbow that smelled like molasses and magic. From the moment we walked through the bright white double doors of the distillery and gift shop, we were greeted with smiling faces and the upbeat energy of our fantastic guide, Christina. She made sure no glass went empty, no fact went untold—and let's be honest, no one left sober.

Unlike anything you'd find back home in Newfoundland, Toppers is both a rum factory and a flavour explosion. With dozens of colourful bottles lining the walls—from coconut cream to jalapeño lime—you're encouraged to try them all, I did and failed miserably. Of course some are part of my private collection.

# RUMgatta: Where the Wind Blows and the Rum Flows

If you ever find yourself in Saint Martin in early March, there's one event you simply can't miss—the St. Maarten Heineken Regatta. It's the largest sailing race in the Caribbean and brings together over a hundred boats from around the world for four thrilling days on the turquoise sea. But this isn't just about the racing—it's also about the "Serious Fun" that happens every night with concerts, beach parties, and ice-cold Heineken flowing like water. The energy is electric, the sails are massive, and the island feels more alive than ever. Crews in costume pass through the bridge like a floating parade, and the whole island joins in the celebration. It's part sport, part spectacle, and all heart. If you're planning a trip to Saint Martin, make sure it's in March. You'll have an unbelievable experience of sites, music, food, people, cultural, and yes sailing.

Over on the French side, Orient Bay offers turquoise waters, white sand, and a little something extra — it's the island's most famous nude beach. You'll find power sailing, incredible food right on the sand, and the freedom to work on your all-over tan. I wouldn't know firsthand, of course… I must've just heard that from a friend.

## Final Thoughts

It may not be the fanciest rum. It may not win gold medals.

But in a world of boring branding and copycat labels, Big Black Dick stands tall—and leaves a lasting impression it's rum that I will never forget

CHAPTER 14

# Rum Roads & Wrong Turns in Anguilla

While in Saint Martin, I hopped on a quick 30-minute ferry across turquoise waters and landed in Anguilla—one of the most peaceful, postcard-perfect places I've ever visited. Tranquil, friendly, and lined with some of the most beautiful beaches in the world, it felt like stepping into a slower, better version of time.

Naturally, I rented a scooter. And naturally, I forgot they drive on the opposite side of the road. It wasn't long before a car came straight at me, horns blaring, while I waved politely and pretended this was all part of my "island tour package." Once I got my bearings (and my heart out of my throat), I cruised straight to a rum lover's paradise—the legendary Zemi Beach House.

There, tucked inside this beachfront gem, is the Rhum Room—home to over 90 premium rums from across the globe. The ambiance was elegant but relaxed, and the staff knew their stuff. Of course, they featured their own local favourite: Pyrat Rum, that used to be bottled right there in Anguilla. Smooth, spicy, and served with a view that made you want to stay forever.

As I sat there sipping a flight of rums, waves rolling just outside and the warm breeze blowing in, I looked at the man behind the bar—and it hit me. That guy had my perfect life. My dream job. He was running an incredible rum bar on a tranquil beach, serving up liquid sunshine and giving every tourist a little rum education with a smile. That was it—he was living the dream. And for a brief moment, I considered never going home. While in Anguilla, I picked up two bottles of Pyrat Rum—now produced and bottled in Guyana. Although production has moved, the spirit of Pyrat still lingers on the island. Anguillans speak of it with a sense of pride and nostalgia, having once been home to its bottling. That connection lives on in the bars and beach shacks, where you'll still find Pyrat poured with reverence—and maybe even a little local legend.

The food? Incredible. The beaches? Flawless. The rum? Flowing.

It was only a few days, but Anguilla left a lasting mark—on my heart, my taste buds, and nearly the front of that car.

> **How do you turn water into rum?**
> **Be born in the Caribbean and pray you're lucky.**

CHAPTER 15

# Sailor Jerry and Tattoos at Sea

Long before his name was on a bottle, Sailor Jerry was known for something far more permanent than a hangover—tattoos. And not just any tattoos—he practically invented the classic naval tattoo style still worn proudly today by sailors, rebels, bikers, and bartenders.

But how did a legendary tattoo artist become the face of one of the most recognizable spiced rums on Earth?

Let's talk ink, attitude, and alcohol.

## Who Was Sailor Jerry?

Born Norman Keith Collins in 1911, he later became known as Sailor Jerry, a name earned while serving in the U.S. Navy. He traveled the Pacific, studied Japanese tattooing, and eventually opened a tattoo shop in Honolulu, Hawaii, which became the place to get inked for sailors on shore leave during WWII.

His style?

Bold lines. Bright colours. Anchors, hula girls, eagles, skulls, snakes, and of course—pin-up girls.

His work was gritty, patriotic, and wildly popular.

Jerry didn't just tattoo—he revolutionized the craft. He invented new pigments, sterilization techniques, and electric needle modifications. He brought respectability and artistry to what was once seen as a fringe trade. If you were in the navy, you wore his tattoos with pride.

## The Rum Comes Later

After his death in 1973, Sailor Jerry's legacy lived on through his protégés, who kept his flash art and spirit alive. In the early 2000s, a group of entrepreneurs licensed his brand and launched Sailor Jerry Spiced Rum—infused with vanilla, cinnamon, clove, and plenty of swagger.

It was a boozy tribute to the man, the myth, the ink.

The bottles featured his original tattoo artwork—especially the pin-up girls that made him famous. Some bottles even had hidden peel-off tattoos inside the label, and limited editions included sailor sayings and flash art.

## Tattoos, Tradition, and Toughness

In the Navy, tattoos weren't just decoration—they were rites of passage. A swallow on the chest meant 5,000 nautical miles. A hula girl meant you'd been to Hawaii. And Sailor Jerry's art became badges of honour across the globe.

Men would line up outside his shop, sometimes waiting hours, to get tattooed before shipping out. For some, it was a way to feel brave. For others, it was a way to be remembered if they didn't make it home.

## Why the Rum Works

Sailor Jerry rum isn't fancy—it's bold, spicy, and unapologetic. It tastes like cannon fire, feels like a back tattoo, and doesn't try to be something it's not.

It's the kind of rum you drink with your crew.

The kind of bottle you keep for the stories.

And the kind of brand that reminds you that some legends never die—they just get bottled.

# Collector Photos From My Rum Room Collection

1. "Snake Charmer" – Woman kneeling with a snake and flute.

2. "Peacock Pin-Up" – Woman with a peacock feather fan.

3. "Purple Temptress" – Classic pin-up pose in a deep violet outfit.

1. "Navy Girl" – Woman in sailor uniform with a white top and miniskirt.

2. "Eastern Elegance" – Woman in a patterned cheongsam-style dress.

3. "Lucky Lady" – Pin-up with a banner reading "Lucky" and roses (a classic tattoo design).

What's a pirate's least favourite letter?
A DWI.

CHAPTER 16

# Bacardi – Bats, Revolution, and a Family Legacy

You'll find Bacardi behind almost every bar in the world. It's one of the biggest rum brands of all time—synonymous with cocktails like the Cuba Libre, Mojito, and Daiquiri. But behind the white label and flying bat lies one of the wildest survival stories in rum history.

Because Bacardi didn't just build a brand.

They built an empire. And then they lost it—and kept going.

## It All Started With a Bat

In 1862, Don Facundo Bacardí Massó, a Spanish wine merchant living in Cuba, decided to try his hand at rum. Up until then, Cuban rum was rough—think fuel for pirates. But Don Facundo refined the process, charcoal-filtered it, aged it in oak, and created a smoother, more elegant spirit.

His wife spotted a colony of fruit bats in the rafters of the first distillery. In Cuban and Taino culture, bats were symbols of health, prosperity, and family unity—so they made it the company logo. Bacardi's iconic journey began in Santiago de Cuba in 1862, when Don Facundo Bacardí Massó purchased his first distillery for 500 pesos—a modest sum at the time, which would be roughly $20–25 USD back then (equivalent to several hundred dollars today when adjusted for inflation).

To this day, the bat is Bacardi's most recognizable symbol.

## The Rise of a Cuban Powerhouse

Bacardi quickly became Cuba's rum of choice. It was classy, consistent, and came in stylish bottles. By the early 1900s, Bacardi had grown into a juggernaut with distilleries, bars, and offices in Havana, New York, and Spain.

The Cuba Libre (rum and Coke with lime) was born during the Spanish-American War. The Daiquiri became Hemingway's favourite drink. Bacardi was everywhere.

But then came revolution.

Fidel Castro and the Fall of an Empire

In 1959, Fidel Castro's revolution changed everything. Bacardi had been a vocal opponent of communism, and when Castro came to power, he seized all private businesses, including the Bacardi family's distilleries, offices, and trademarks within Cuba.

They lost everything—overnight.

But here's where the story gets good.

The Bacardi family had already moved some of their assets abroad. They had distilleries in Puerto Rico and Mexico, trademarks secured in the U.S., and their top executives had flown out just before the takeover. In true rum-runner style, they survived by planning ahead.

Bacardi Limited now operates more than 20 distilleries, bottling facilities, and production sites worldwide.

## The Exile Legacy

Bacardi rebuilt from the ashes—outside of Cuba.

They sued the Cuban government, waged a decades-long legal war over trademarks, and continued to market their rum as "The Spirit of Cuba"— even though it's been made outside Cuba since 1960.

Today, Bacardi is still family-owned, headquartered in Bermuda, and produces over 200 million bottles of rum per year.

## More Than Just a Brand

Bacardi isn't just about sales. It's about resilience.

They lost their homeland, their properties, and their founding distillery— but they never lost their identity.

Every bottle still carries the bat, every cocktail still tells their story, and every sip is a reminder that some spirits are too strong to kill.

> Why do Newfoundlanders keep rum in the freezer?
> In case the power goes out, they don't want to lose the essentials.

CHAPTER 17

# Lamb's Rum and Newfoundland Pride

If you grew up on the Rock, chances are your first real drink—or at least your first real hangover—involved Lamb's Rum. Whether it was Lamb's Navy, Lamb's Spiced, or a splash of it in a Coke at a kitchen party, this rum has been a Newfoundland staple for generations.

But how did a British navy rum become the drink of choice for an island half a world away?

## From London to St. John's

Lamb's Rum was originally blended in London in 1849 by Alfred Lamb, a 22-year-old merchant with a keen nose and a sailor's heart. He crafted a dark navy-style rum using spirits from Guyana, Trinidad, and Jamaica—a blend rich in molasses, smoke, and tradition.

It became the go-to rum for the British Royal Navy, and as Britain's empire expanded, so did Lamb's.

Eventually, it found a home in Newfoundland—where the cold winds, long winters, and salt-hardened people took to it like cod to a boat.

## Wince Worthman: The Man Who Brought Lamb's to Newfoundland

In the early 1960s, Wince Worthman, a savvy liquor agent from Newfoundland, recognized the potential of Lamb's Rum for the local market. He secured the rights to distribute Lamb's in the province, introducing it to a population that quickly embraced it as their own. Worthman's efforts were instrumental in establishing Lamb's as a staple in Newfoundland's liquor landscape, where it remains a beloved brand to this day.

Source: https://www.cbc.ca/news/canada/newfoundland-labrador/wince-worthman-lambs-1.4570326

Because I spent years on George Street and other bars around the island, I had the pleasure of meeting Wince Worthman—doing a few deals with him and sharing a proper Newfoundland toast. A true legend in the rum world, Wince helped shape Newfoundland's modern rum legacy with the same spirit that built our province—bold, resilient, and just a little bit wild.

## Why Newfoundland Loves It

Let's be honest: Newfoundlanders don't mess around when it comes to drinking. The culture runs deep—from baymen to townies, from jigging on the wharf to dancing at the Legion hall. And Lamb's was always part of that scene.

Over 100,000 cases sold every year in Newfoundland. Representing 23% of spirit sales in the province.

It was affordable, reliable, and strong.
The perfect bottle for:
- Screech in
- Cabin parties
- Weddings
- Wakes
- Or just a midweek "I made it through the day" drink

It's not fancy. It doesn't try to be.

And that's exactly why we love it.

# A Tribute to Dawn Collier: A Woman Who Could Drink Most Men Under the Table

When I first met Dawn Collier, we worked in housing together for years—and let me tell you, we did more evictions than some provinces do in a year. At one point, I thought we should've been issued badges, black trench coats, and our own theme music. If there was a Guinness World Record for "fastest lock change and notice served," we'd be holding the title and toasting it with a rum.

Now let me tell you about Dawn Collier—a woman with class, danger, and rare talent, all rolled into one. Dawn was the kind of Newfoundlander who could drink any man under the table, put him to shame, and then politely excuse herself and head to bed early, just to remind you she still had manners.

One night, we were out in a garage—because that's where all great the Newfoundland parties happen—and she offered me a drink. I thought, sure, why not? But by the second one, my legs got wobbly, my eyes started seeing things, and I was questioning reality.

I turned to her and said, "Dawn, what did you put in this?"

She looked at me, cool as ever, and said, "What's wrong with you, maid? Same as I always do—50/50."

Now, let's do the math together. It was an 8-ounce glass. That means 4 ounces of rum in each drink. Two drinks? That's 8 ounces of rum—and with Dawn's heavy pour, it may have been more like a Newfoundland tide rolling in.

The last thing I remember was eating something that might have been Chinese food, and then stumbling home like I'd just returned from war. I never dared return… except for jigs dinner, of course. Because no matter how dangerous the night was, you don't skip out on a feed like that.

Newfoundlanders don't need fancy labels. We just need a good poor good story a little something to keep the cold out and of course jigs dinner.

> **What's a Newfoundlander's idea of moderation?**
> **One bottle per hand.**

CHAPTER 18

# The Smuggler's Spirit – Kirk and Sweeney Rum

## From Rumrunner to Rum Royalty

Not every great rum enters your life through duty-free shops or tropical getaways—sometimes it shows up at your door in Fort McMurray, Alberta.

When a Mr. Mikes Steakhouse was opening in town, I had the chance to meet the actual owner of the brand. Somehow, word had gotten to him that I was a bit of a rum man. Now, I don't know if it was the twinkle in his eye or the subtle rattle in the bottle bag, but he showed up with a gift: a squat, rounded bottle labeled Kirk and Sweeney 12-Year-Old Dominican Rum.

The bottle was unique—shaped like an old-fashioned decanter, with a map etched into the glass and a name I didn't recognize. That night, we cracked it open, and from the first sip, I knew this wasn't just another dark liquor. It was smooth, rich, and full of character—much like the stories behind it.

And that's where my research began.

## The History Behind the Name

Kirk and Sweeney was no ordinary name—it belonged to an actual rum-running schooner that gained notoriety during Prohibition. Built in Gloucester, Massachusetts, the real Kirk and Sweeney smuggled rum from the Caribbean up the East Coast of the U.S., often hovering just outside American waters as part of what was known as "Rum Row."

In 1924, the U.S. Coast Guard intercepted the schooner off the coast of New York with thousands of cases of rum onboard. She was seized, her crew arrested, and her legend born. While the Coast Guard called it justice, others called it a damn shame.

## Dominican Craftsmanship in a Yankee Name

Though the name is rooted in New England's rum-running past, the liquid inside is pure Dominican artistry. Distilled in Santiago de los Caballeros, this rum is aged in American oak barrels for a full 12 years using sugarcane molasses and traditional aging techniques.

It's made at one of the most respected distilleries in the Dominican Republic, long connected to the Barceló family—a name that carries weight in the Caribbean rum world.

"Kirk and Sweeney 12-Year – From a Prohibition schooner to my shelf in Fort McMurray, courtesy of a steakhouse and a hunch."

Kirk and Sweeney XO – Edición Limitada Nº 2 in a luxurious wooden box with gold lettering – a standout in my collector series

Tasting Notes (Kirk and Sweeney 12-Year)

- Nose: Burnt sugar, vanilla bean, oak, and dried apricot
- Palate: Rich molasses, caramel, toffee, with undertones of roasted nuts and spice
- Finish: Long, warm, and slightly smoky—just enough to make you pour a second glass

This is sipping rum at its finest—best enjoyed neat, or maybe with one cube, if you're being fancy.

## Legacy and What It Means to Me

That bottle opened more than just a cork—it opened a door into the rum-running world I'd never fully explored. From a steakhouse handshake in Alberta to the sugarcane fields of the Dominican Republic and the rogue schooners of the Atlantic, Kirk and Sweeney connected continents, cultures, and now, my own curiosity.

It was proof that good rum has a way of finding the right people, even if you're a thousand miles from the nearest tropical beach.

> "The Kirk and Sweeney used to smuggle barrels of rum into New York. Now I smuggle it into my living room—no Coast Guard, no questions asked. Just a glass and good company."

CHAPTER 19

# The Prince to Peddler Program – COVID, Curried Goat, and Chairman's Reserve

Before the world shut down, Prince—a good friend of mine—was a regular visitor to St. Lucia, making trips back and forth with his family. Every time he returned, he'd bring me a bottle of Chairman's Reserve, one of the island's finest rums.

He knew I loved it. And I knew I could count on him.

But when COVID hit, everything changed.

## Grounded in St. Lucia

When the pandemic struck, borders closed and airlines went dark. Prince's wife and kids got stuck in St. Lucia, unable to come home. He was still in Canada, juggling work, life, and trying to figure out how to get his family back safely.

But even during the chaos, one tradition didn't stop—the rum order.

Every time Prince got wind of a possible flight or cargo connection, I'd say the same thing:

"If you're bringing your family back... don't forget the Chairman's!"

## The Backyard Economy

With restaurants shut down and stores picked clean, we did what Newfoundlanders and West Indians have always done in hard times: we bartered.

I started cooking up massive pots of curried goat, oxtail, and jerk chicken in my backyard. Friends and neighbours would come by—socially distanced, of course—and we'd trade food, drinks, and stories like the old days.

Prince, true to his name, always showed up with a bottle.

And thus, the "Prince to Peddler Program," was born.

## From a Prince to a Peddler

It wasn't official, but it worked.

Rum moved through back fences. Plates of steaming goat were passed with elbow bumps. Nobody kept score. Nobody asked for change.

We just shared what we had—and what we loved.

When Prince finally arranged a charter flight to get his wife and

**Curry goat cooked in the garden**

**Jerk chicken with Chairman Reserve Rum**

kids home, it felt like a victory. Not just for his family, but for the bond that had grown stronger during a time when the world felt uncertain.

Of course, I made sure he didn't step foot on that tarmac until I had one more bottle of Chairman's Reserve in hand.

## The Spirit of the Story

This wasn't just about rum.

It was about community, culture, and connection—the kind you can't buy at the liquor store or bottle up on a shelf.

To this day, when I pour a glass of Chairman's, I think of those pandemic nights under the stars, a pot bubbling over fire, and a man doing everything he could for his family… with a bottle in his hand and a plate in his lap.

> A woman by the name of Mary got a call from Newfoundland and Labrador liquor corporation with some terrible news. Her husband fell into a vat of screech and died. The wife was shocked and asked did he die instantly. No, the man on the other end of the phone said he got out twice for a pee.

CHAPTER 20

# Brazil's Cachaça vs. Rum – Juice or Molasses?

Most of the world knows rum as a sweet, golden spirit born from molasses—a byproduct of refining sugarcane. But in Brazil, they took a different route. Instead of using what's left behind, they went straight for the source: fresh-pressed sugarcane juice. The result? A fiery, earthy, and utterly unique spirit known as cachaça (pronounced ka-SHA-sa). My first bottle was given to me in Fort McMurray by a great Masonic brother by the name of Dale Penny.

And while some folks lump it in with rum, Brazilians would kindly (or not so kindly) remind you:

"Cachaça is not rum. Cachaça is Brazil."

## What's the Difference?

- Rum is typically made from molasses, which gives it a rich, smooth, caramel flavour.
- Cachaça, on the other hand, is made from fresh sugarcane juice, distilled quickly after pressing. The taste is often grassy, herbal, with a sharp bite—like a sugarcane field in a bottle.

In terms of culture, the two spirits couldn't be more different. While rum is steeped in pirate tales, naval traditions, and colonial export, cachaça is local, wild, and passionate—deeply tied to Brazil's Afro-Indigenous roots and working-class pride.

Cachaça was first distilled in the 1500s by enslaved Africans on Portuguese plantations—making it one of the oldest distilled spirits in the Americas. Unlike rum, which was often exported, cachaça stayed at home and became central to Brazilian celebrations, especially in the country's most beloved drink: the Caipirinha (lime, sugar, ice, and cachaça—simple and deadly).

Today, Brazil produces over 1.5 billion litres of cachaça each year, and while the world is only just catching on, it remains a source of national pride. There are even festivals devoted to it—complete with samba, BBQ, and enough dancing to shake the sugarcane fields loose.

So next time you raise a glass of rum, remember its Brazilian cousin. And if someone hands you a shot of cachaça and says,

"Saúde!"

You better sip it slowly… or risk dancing on the table.

## A Spirit of the People

Cachaça dates back to the 1500s, making it one of the oldest distilled spirits in the Americas. Portuguese colonists, enslaved Africans, and Indigenous knowledge all contributed to its production. Over time, it became the spirit of Brazil's working class—the drink of the farm, the favela, and the football pitch.

There are over 4,000 registered cachaça distilleries in Brazil—many family-run, rustic, and proud.

## Caipirinha: Brazil in a Glass

If you've never had a Caipirinha, stop reading and go make one.

It's simple:

- 1 lime (cut into wedges)
- 2 tsp sugar
- 2 oz cachaça
- Crushed ice

Muddle the lime and sugar. Add cachaça. Ice it up.

I have made this many times in the rum room for guests and always enjoyed (lots of ice).

It's refreshing, strong, and sneaky—you'll be dancing samba before you finish the second one.

## So… Is It Rum?

Technically, cachaça could be classified as a type of rum under international standards. But Brazilian law protects the name—just like how Champagne must come from France. And, culturally, cachaça stands on its own.

Where rum whispers of ships, pirates, and ports…

Cachaça sings of beaches, bonfires, and barefoot samba.

So the next time you're holding a bottle of rum, tip your hat to Brazil. Because whether it's molasses or fresh cane, aged in oak or poured straight from the still—the sugarcane spirit world is vast, passionate, and full of surprises

CHAPTER 21

# Haitian Rum — Resilience in a Bottle

Haiti's rum is like the country itself — raw, wild, beautiful, and unbreakable.

While many know of Rhum Barbancourt, the world-class sugarcane juice rum aged in French oak, Haiti's deeper rum story lies in the hills — in the rustic, handmade spirit called clairin. With over 500 micro-distilleries scattered across the countryside, clairin is distilled the old-fashioned way:

- No molasses. No additives.
- Fermented with wild airborne yeast
- Fired with leftover crushed cane (bagasse)
- Distilled in wood-fired pot stills, often using tools passed down through generations

*Rhum Barbancourt (see how labeling changed on boxes over 10 years).*

Each clairin is a snapshot of the land — from the sugarcane to the water to the hands that make it. Distilleries like Clairin Sajous, Casimir, Vaval, and Le Rocher have achieved cult status globally for their bold, funky profiles and raw authenticity.

But the miracle? They're still making it — even now.

Since the assassination of President Jovenel Moïse in July 2021, Haiti has been without an elected president. In 2024, Prime Minister Ariel Henry resigned, and a Transitional Presidential Council took control amid violence and unrest. Elections are tentatively planned for 2026, but the path is uncertain.

Yet through it all — the gang blockades, blackouts, and political collapse — the rum has never stopped.

Even when streets burn, distillers in the mountains still light fires under copper stills, crush cane by hand, and bottle what some call the purest expression of Caribbean spirit.

"Governments collapse. Hope fades. But in Haiti, rum endures — because it is the soul of the people in liquid form."

> They told me the rum was aged 12 years. I said, 'Perfect, same as my maturity level.

# PART III

# Rum Across The Map

CHAPTER 22

# The Rocky Mountain Rum-Runners – Crowsnest Pass and the Alberta Connection

## From the Rock to the Rockies – Rum Has a Way of Travelling

As a proud Newfoundlander now living in Alberta, it didn't take long before I found myself digging into the history of this province's own rum-running past. And let me tell you, just like back home, the mountains have their secrets—and in southern Alberta's Crowsnest Pass; they whisper the tales of barrels, bullets, and bootleggers.

## Prohibition and the Rise of Rum-Running

In 1916, Alberta jumped headfirst into Prohibition, banning the sale and consumption of alcohol. But much like the rest of Canada (and certainly Newfoundland), the thirst didn't dry up just because the law said so. In the mining towns of the Crowsnest Pass, Blairmore, Coleman, Bellevue, and Hillcrest, workers still craved their post-shift relief, and where there's demand, there's always someone ready to supply.

Enter the rum-runners.

With British Columbia just over the mountain and the U.S. not far south, Crowsnest Pass became the perfect funnel for illegal liquor. Higher-quality spirits were smuggled across provincial and international borders, a step above your garden-variety moonshine bootlegged out back. The smugglers were savvy, gutsy, and fast, relying on mountain trails, hidden compartments, and sometimes a good bribe or two to keep the flow going.

## Emilio Picariello: The "Bottle King" of the Pass

No story of Alberta rum-running is complete without Emilio Picariello, a man who might as well be Alberta's answer to Al Capone with a bit more class and a whole lot more snow.

An Italian immigrant and entrepreneur, Picariello owned the Alberta Hotel in Blairmore. Officially, he sold ice and cigars. Unofficially, he moved a lot of liquor. He ran a tight operation, even building a tunnel under the street to sneak bottles from his hotel to delivery wagons without ever stepping into daylight. The man had ambition and a nose for opportunity.

But ambition in the age of Prohibition came at a cost.

## The Tragic Confrontation

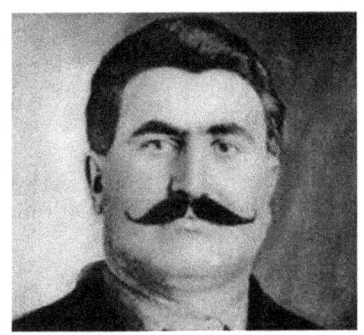

In September 1922, things took a dark turn. Picariello's son, Steve, was shot and wounded by Alberta Provincial Police Constable Stephen Lawson during a conflict. Enraged, Emilio, along with his close associate Florence Lassandro, confronted Lawson at the APP barracks in Coleman.

What happened next shocked the country.

Lawson was shot and killed in the street. Picariello and Lassandro were arrested, tried, and convicted of murder. Both were executed in 1923 at the Fort Saskatchewan jail, making Lassandro the first and only woman ever hanged in Alberta. Some say she pulled the trigger; others say she took the fall. Either way, she became a tragic figure in the story of Prohibition's grip on the Canadian West.

## Legacy and Remembrance

Today, the story of Crowsnest Pass lives on not just in whispers or in glass bottles dug up from cellars, but in preserved sites and interpretive displays. The APP barracks in Coleman is now a museum where visitors can explore the full story of Picariello, Lassandro, and the outlaw trade that once surged through these mountain towns.

The legacy is one of contradiction: law vs. livelihood, survival vs. sacrifice, and a whole lot of gray in between. Just like in Newfoundland, the fight against rum was never really about the bottle—it was about control, culture, and the courage of everyday people caught in the middle.

> How do you know a Newfoundlander is at the bar?
> He's buying drinks for people he hasn't even met yet.

CHAPTER 23

# Romero Distilling – Rum, Rhymes, and the Spirit of Crowsnest Pass

## From the Rockies to the Bottle – A Legacy Reborn

Not many rum distilleries can claim their roots are tangled in gunfights, smuggling tunnels, and a woman's last dance before the gallows. But in Calgary, Alberta, one distillery is proudly bottling that very legacy.

Romero Distilling Co. was founded with the mission to tell the untold story of Alberta's rum-running past—a story that comes alive in the Crowsnest Pass, where Emilio Picariello and Florence Lassandro were caught smuggling booze during Prohibition. Their story ended in tragedy, but the spirit of what they started now lives on in every sip of Romero rum.

## A Visit to Remember – Rum and Cabaret

I had the chance to visit Romero Distilling myself—and let me tell you, this wasn't your average tasting room. The place was alive with cabaret-style entertainment, laughter, music, and people who clearly knew their spirits.

The owner, himself, greeted me and immediately launched into a poetic explanation of rum, distillation, and the science behind every bottle. He talked about:

- Heads, hearts, and tails in the distillation process—how only the "hearts" are kept for top-quality rum
- The fermentation techniques they use with molasses sourced from the best sugarcane
- The difference between a spirit and a rum, based on aging and ingredients
- And the aging process in oak barrels, which imparts colour, flavour, and complexity

It wasn't just education—it was entertainment, Alberta-style. And, of course, about $1,000 and several bottles later, I left with a collection I was proud to add to my shelf.

## The Bottles in My Collection

Romero Amber and Spiced Rum – Alberta's only rum-dedicated distillery, where the bootleg past meets craft perfection. In my photo, you'll see two standout selections:

- Romero Amber Rum (Rhum Ambré) – Smooth, warm, and balanced with notes of caramel, vanilla, and subtle oak.
- Romero Spiced Rum (Rhum Épicé) – A local take on Caribbean spice, with cinnamon, nutmeg, and just enough kick to remind you that you're in the Rockies, not the islands.

Both bottles proudly say on the label:

"Building on the largely untold history of rum running in Alberta, Canada."

And they do exactly that—with taste, honour, and a little bit of wild west spirit.

## Why Romero Matters

Romero Distilling is the only craft distillery in Alberta dedicated solely to rum. Most Canadian distilleries focus on whisky, vodka, or gin—but Romero said to hell with that and leaned into molasses and Prohibition legends.

They're not just crafting rum—they're bottling Alberta's forgotten stories.

"They say rum used to be smuggled into Alberta under cover of night—now it's sold in broad daylight with a live jazz band and better lighting."

## CHAPTER 24

# "Brum" with a View – A Toast to Rig Hand and a Good Buddy

I first heard about Rig Hand Distillery from my good friend Kirk Soroka—a long-time military veteran, fighter pilot, and storyteller who's looked down on more history than most of us have read in books. The man has seen the world from a cockpit, but when it comes to Alberta, his boots are planted firmly in the ground.

We met at work and hit it off fast. A couple of months later, we showed up at Rig Hand with our better halves—two women who are both far too classy to hang out with the likes of us. It turned into one of those evenings you don't forget: amazing food, a full tour of the facility, and a crash course in how they make everything from vodka to whisky—and what we thought was rum.

Except… it wasn't quite rum.

It's called "Brum."

Now Kirk was the one who said it best, with that half-smirk he gets when he's about to drop a truth bomb:

"It ain't rum… but it drinks like one—and it's got more grit than most men I've flown with."

And he wasn't wrong.

Brum isn't made with molasses or sugarcane. It's made with Alberta-grown sugar beets, the same kind of harvest that built this province. It may look like rum, pour like rum, and feel like rum—but it's 100% homegrown prairie spirit. You could almost taste the wheat fields and welding torches in every sip.

We left that night with full bellies, a couple bottles, and a great memory.

Rig Hand feels like stepping onto an old western movie set—wood beams, fireside chats, and views of Saunders Lake. They've got a dog-friendly patio, live music, lawn games, and probably more fun per square foot than most airports... and they're only 4KM from one.

The place is also a salute to every hard-working Albertan. Everyone who comes into our oil camp shows up in lifted F-350s, mud-covered work trucks, and big rigs that smell like diesel and dust. But last time Kirk showed up for lunch, he didn't bother with wheels—he came in by helicopter. Landed like it was just another Tuesday.

So here's to Rig Hand, to the proud legacy of Alberta's oil and agriculture... and to friends like Kirk Soroka, who knows a good drink, a good meal, and a damn good entrance when he sees one.

And that "Brum?" It might not be rum by name—but it was made with sugar beets, boldness, and two beautiful women who made the whole night unforgettable.

Their main sugar beet supplier is Schneider Farms, a fourth-generation family farm just two miles from the distillery. You can taste the local pride in every pour.

This isn't just a distillery—it's Alberta in a bottle. Made for the men and women who build, drill, weld, and feed the world. Poured with purpose, and best shared with someone who knows what it means to earn their sip.

> Buddy said this rum was smooth... "it was so smooth I woke up wearing someone else's rubber boots."

CHAPTER 25

# U.S. Military in Newfoundland – Coca-Cola, Rum, and Culture Clash

During the Second World War, Newfoundland became a strategic stronghold for Allied forces—especially the Americans. Between air bases, naval stations, and thousands of soldiers stationed on the Rock, it was a time of booming construction, culture shock, and more than a few unexpected influences.

And in the middle of it all?

Rum and Coca-Cola.

## "When the Yanks Came Over"

With the 1941 signing of the Lend-Lease Agreement, the U.S. established military bases in places like Argentia, Stephenville, Gander, and Goose Bay. They brought money, machinery, and manpower—and suddenly, small Newfoundland towns were filled with thousands of American GIs.

Local businesses flourished. Roads were built. Dance halls opened. And rum? Well... it met Coca-Cola for the first time.

## Coca-Cola: The Other Invasion

The Americans didn't just bring tanks—they brought Coke.

Before the war, Coca-Cola was almost unknown in Newfoundland. But the U.S. military considered it a morale booster, so they shipped it in by the crate. Soldiers drank it like water. Before long, Newfoundlanders were hooked, too.

It didn't take long before someone said,

"What if we mix this Yankee pop with a bottle of Lamb's?"

And just like that, the Newfoundland Rum and Coke was born.

## Rum, Romance, and Resentment

With American soldiers came romance, and not everyone was thrilled.

Newfoundland women were courted with chocolate bars, nylons, and dances to swing music.

Newfoundland men—especially those still struggling through post-Depression times—weren't impressed.

Tensions rose in some towns, leading to scraps, stories, and more than a few broken bottles. But over time, most Newfoundlanders adapted. Many marriages were formed, and entire communities grew up around the old American bases.

## A Legacy That Lingers

Even after the Americans pulled out, their presence left a lasting mark:

- Rum and Coke became a go-to drink across the island.
- Coca-Cola became a local grocery store staple.
- And some base infrastructure still exists today.

But more importantly, it fused cultures—blending Newfoundland resilience with American rhythm, creating a wartime cocktail of survival, celebration, and the odd fistfight.

More than five billion bottles of Coke were distributed to soldiers during World War II, thanks to Coca-Cola. So next time you sip a Rum and Coke, remember:

It's not just a drink—it's a story in a glass, where war, whiskey, and women danced to Glenn Miller under a starlit Newfoundland sky.

> I told my doctor I only drink rum on special occasions…
> So now I celebrate things like Wednesday, finding matching socks, and remembering my password.
> They serve rum, fish stories, and regrets—usually in that order.

CHAPTER 26

# Al Capone and Rum in St. Pierre & Miquelon

## My First Visit to Saint Pierre – French Rum & Fences

My first visit to Saint Pierre et Miquelon was on a Rotary exchange trip, and stepping off the boat felt like I'd landed smack in the middle of France. Customs officers, gendarmes, and police dogs were waiting at the dock like we'd just flown in from Morocco. Très sérieux, b'y.

After dinner at a local French restaurant—I ate way too much, as usual—I went for a solo stroll to walk it off. When I returned to the hotel, I realized nobody had given me a room key. Everything was locked up tight, like Fort Knox with better bread.

There I was, 6'4", 280 pounds, dressed head to toe in black like a funeral bouncer, trying to scale concrete fences, spot an emergency ladder, and—by the grace of God—find any way inside. Let me be clear: I was not built to be a ninja. I had my room key, the hotel owner had forgotten the key for the main door (I found this out out when I tried to open the door). I walked three miles to the police station, where I had no luck, so I called the hotel. I did everything I could. But everything was locked up tight, like Fort Knox, but even better.

Eventually, I managed to haul myself in through a side window, but not before waking half the town. Turns out the windows were wide open upstairs (third floor). At breakfast the next morning, our district governor stood up, clearly unimpressed, and asked, "Did anyone else hear someone yelling outside for two or three hours last night?" I just quietly buttered my croissant and said nothing. So much for Service Above Self—not one of my fellow Rotarians even checked!

But hey—on the bright side, I did discover some amazing French rum on that trip. So if you ever find yourself locked out in a tux in the middle of the night, just remember: concrete fences can be climbed, grace is real, and French rum is smooth enough to make it all worth it.

## The French Connection

During American Prohibition (1920–1933), alcohol was illegal in the U.S., but it was business as usual in nearby St. Pierre and Miquelon. As French territory, the islands legally imported wine, brandy, Champagne—and most importantly—Caribbean rum.

Capone saw an opportunity.

He (and many other gangsters) used St. Pierre as a storage and staging ground. Massive warehouses were filled with booze, and from there, rum was smuggled into the U.S. and Canada aboard small boats, often under cover of night or fog.

PHOTO OF HOTEL THAT AL CAPONE USED TO STAY IN AND STILL EXISTS TODAY

One warehouse was said to be so full of rum that if you tapped a barrel the wrong way, you could get drenched.

## Rum, Romance, and Real Estate

It's rumored that Capone had real estate holdings on the island, and would occasionally send trusted men to oversee operations. He was even known to visit discreetly—not in pinstripe suits, but dressed down to avoid attention.

The locals knew what was going on, of course—but business was booming.

Bars, hotels, and shipping companies thrived. One islander later said,

"We never made more money than when the world was trying to stay sober."

## Why St. Pierre Worked So Well

- Proximity: Just 25 km from Newfoundland
- Legal loophole: As French territory, they could import and export freely
- Harbour access: Ideal for covert shipping
- Local cooperation: Many islanders were more than happy to play their part

The island's economy boomed—temporarily becoming the richest per capita place in the North Atlantic.

## When Prohibition Ended… So Did the Party

In 1933, the U.S. lifted Prohibition, and the rumrunners' golden age began to fade. St. Pierre's warehouses emptied. The gangsters vanished. And the island slipped back into quiet anonymity.

But the legacy remains.

Today, you can still visit St. Pierre and Miquelon and walk the same streets Al Capone's rum runners did, hear the stories in local bars, and imagine the days when barrels of contraband lined the docks—and rum was the real currency of the island.

Long before credit cards and cell service reached the outports, Newfoundlanders were already mastering the art of international trade—one barrel of rum at a time.

During the American Prohibition, the rugged coast of Newfoundland became a hotbed for rum smuggling. With its thick fog, endless coves, and close proximity to St. Pierre and Miquelon (France's tiny liquor-soaked island), the island was perfectly positioned to become the East Coast's rum highway.

And oh boy, did it deliver.

## St. Pierre and Miquelon – The Wettest Neighbour Ever

Ships and skiffs would leave Newfoundland under cover of darkness or misty mornings, head for St. Pierre, load up with French brandy, Caribbean rum, and European wine, and be back before the sun burned off the fog. The locals called it "going for groceries."

Some say entire church groups were in on it. Others say the church blessed the shipments. Either way, rum got through.

## Smuggling with Style (and a Bit of Sarcasm)

Unlike the gangsters of Chicago, Newfoundland's rum runners were more… resourceful than ruthless. Fish boats were converted into cargo vessels. Barrels were hidden under nets, inside herring barrels, or even disguised as cod oil.

Local policemen knew what was happening—and often had a bottle or two themselves. One famous story tells of a Mountie who asked, "What's in the barrel, boy?" The fisherman replied,

"Just bait, sir. If you'd like to sample it, I'll pour you a shot."

## The Legends, the Laughs, and the Legacy

Some rum runners became folk heroes—like the man who outran a government boat by tossing empty barrels into the water to slow the chase. Or the woman who baked rum cakes as a cover for smuggling... and made a fortune.

Whole communities depended on the extra income from "the trade." It wasn't seen as crime—it was just survival with a splash of cleverness.

Even after Prohibition ended in the U.S., the tradition lived on. St. Pierre remained a party destination. Newfoundland's love affair with rum only grew stronger, leading to iconic brands like Lamb's Rum becoming a household name (very similar to Aunt Martha's sheep and the Mountie are the most) for you come from aways (Google it to understand).

## A Rum Legacy Etched in Rock

To this day, if you walk the docks or share a drink in a Newfoundland pub, you'll hear whispers of those days—stories told with pride, humour, and maybe a wink. Because in Newfoundland, rum running wasn't just history.

It was a family business, a community effort and a damn good reason to raise a glass.

> Why don't Newfoundlanders ever get lost at sea?
> Because wherever they go, they bring rum and end up starting a party.
> You know it's a proper St. John's weekend when your hangover needs its own day off.

CHAPTER 27

# From Plantation to Planteray

## A Rum About Diversity

When I started digging deeper into the history of Plantation Rum — the flavour, the roots, and, most of all, the name — I knew exactly who to call.

I had met Guillaume Lamy a few years earlier in Barbados — a man so passionate about rum he could sweat out a tasting note. I remembered the way he spoke about the team, the barrels, the blending, and the future of the spirit like it was something alive and deeply personal.

So, I reached out.

He didn't dodge the question. In fact, he welcomed it. And then, he shared the full story.

The name Plantation had always carried a heavy weight — for obvious reasons. But the decision to move away from it didn't come from public pressure or headlines. It started at a simple staff party at the distillery — a moment of honest connection.

Glasses were clinking, the mood was festive, and Guillaume, always a listener, turned to one of his senior team members and asked:

"Do you have a problem with the name Plantation?"

The answer was immediate:

"Of course we do — it's from slavery."

And just like that, things began to shift. Not with outrage or obligation — but with understanding. The leadership knew that if even one member of the team couldn't fully stand behind the name, the mission was incomplete. This was a company built on showcasing the best of the rum world — and that could only happen if everyone involved felt proud to stand behind the label.

So they made the decision to evolve.

The new name, Planteray, draws from plant and ray — symbolizing the agriculture of cane, the light of the tropics, and the culture of the people who make it all happen. The logo didn't change — it was simply explained: the rays of sunshine surrounding a morphing symbol of a human and a cane. A tribute to both people and process.

The rum? Still the same. Same barrels. Same brilliance. Same beating heart.

This wasn't about erasing the past — it was about honoring the present and building a future that every employee, and every rum lover, could be proud of.

Same damn good rum. Stronger spirit. And one hell of a reason to raise a glass.

*"It wasn't a corporate decision. It was a conversation with family — and doing the right thing."*

— Guillaume Lamy

**Rum in the Caribbean is like oxygen—if you're not using it, you're probably not alive.**

# CHAPTER 28

# My Trip to Barbados – St. Nicholas Abbey, Rum as Religion & West Indies Distillery

If rum had a cathedral, this would be it.

That's what I thought the moment I stepped foot on the grounds of St. Nicholas Abbey in Barbados—a place where time seems to slow down, and rum isn't just a drink… it's a calling.

## A Step Back in Time

St. Nicholas Abbey isn't just a distillery—it's a living, breathing museum of rum history. The estate dates back to 1658, making it one of the oldest surviving plantation houses in the Caribbean.

But this isn't some dusty relic. The abbey has been beautifully preserved, with its original Jacobean architecture, sprawling mahogany trees, and sweeping views over the lush sugarcane fields that still supply its rum today.

Walking through the property, you can feel the past in every creaking floorboard, every brick wall—and every barrel aging quietly in the cellar.

## Copper, Craft, and Caribbean Gold

Then you get to the heart of it: the distillery.

The rum at St. Nicholas Abbey is made with estate-grown sugarcane, crushed on site using a steam-powered mill from 1890. The juice is then slowly fermented, distilled in a copper pot still, and aged in American oak barrels.

I saw it all with my own eyes—and yes; I snapped pictures like a tourist on their honeymoon.

(And maybe I was. A honeymoon with rum.)

# The Shell Chandelier and the Spirit of Place

One of the most breathtaking sights?

A massive chandelier made entirely of seashells, hanging in the Great House like a symbol of both nature and elegance. It's delicate and haunting, and it somehow fits perfectly with the warm Caribbean breeze.

Even the trees on the estate feel like old souls. Some are hundreds of years old, shading the old stone paths with a reverence that's hard to explain.

This wasn't a rum tour.

It was a pilgrimage.

## Tasting the Faith

Of course, the highlight was the tasting.

Their five-year-old rum was floral, rich, and layered with notes of tropical fruit, vanilla, and spice.

The ten-year? Liquid gold.

I bought bottles, took notes, and tried not to cry.

At that moment, I wasn't just sipping rum. I was honouring it.

So yeah, if rum had a cathedral, St. Nicholas Abbey is the altar.

And I walked away a little more faithful, a little more grateful and a whole lot more inspired.

# West Indies Rum Distillery in Barbados

My visit to the West Indies Rum Distillery in Barbados was nothing short of unforgettable. Nestled right along the island's stunning beaches, the salty breeze mingled with the rich, sweet aroma rising from the vats of molasses—it was pure heaven for any rum lover. Guided by none other than the managing director himself, Guillaume Lamy, and his incredible team, we explored the heart of the distillery. We even had the rare privilege of meeting a master blender and getting a sneak peek into their private vault. It wasn't just a tour—it was a journey into the soul of Barbadian rum.

THE BIG BOSS, GUILLAUME LAMY (MANAGING DIRECTOR), OF WEST INDIES DISTILLERY

Another brand they distilled is called Cockspur.

Here's a breakdown of what's in my photo, a beautiful shelf of Stade's Rum—a connoisseur's dream lineup! This brand is a rising star in the rum world, especially among collectors and Master Rummelier circles like yours.

## Stade's Rum – A Modern Tribute to Barbados Heritage

Brand Origin:

Stade's Rum is a premium Barbadian rum brand, produced at the West Indies Rum Distillery (WIRD). It pays homage to the legacy of Mr. Stade, the founder of the distillery in 1893. The brand brings back traditional Barbadian styles using pot and column stills, tropical aging, and authenticity in every bottle.

My Collection Includes:

1. Stade's Rum – Bond No. 8

- Blue and gold label.
- Likely a limited release or a special blend

## Mount Gay – The World's Oldest Rum and A Day to Remember

My visit to Mount Gay in Barbados was nothing short of historic—because this isn't just any distillery, it's the oldest rum distillery in the world, officially dating back to 1703. The moment we arrived, it was clear this was sacred ground for any rum enthusiast. The massive warehouses were stacked high with aging barrels, each one steeped in over three centuries of tradition.

The water that gives Mount Gay its signature character comes from pure underground springs—part of what makes Barbadian rum so distinct. The distillery itself is located near a UNESCO World Heritage Site, and the entire area feels like walking through a living museum of rum history.

We had the incredible fortune of spending the day with the president of the company and their master distillers. They welcomed us like family and took us behind the scenes—from the aging rooms to the fermentation vats, and even out to the sugarcane fields where it all begins. The passion and pride in every person we met was as strong as the rum itself.

Here's a fun fact: Mount Gay's early records were so old they were kept in naval logs. This rum was the favorite of British sailors and was once given as a ration to those brave enough to navigate the Atlantic. Some even say a bottle of Mount Gay has been on every sea worth sailing.

# My Private Stock of Mount Gay Rum

They asked me if I believed in moderation.
I said sure do—moderately full glass of rum at all times.

CHAPTER 29

# Dominican Republic – Ron, Roots, and a Touch of Mamajuana Magic

On my trip to the Dominican Republic last year, I made it my mission to taste every local rum I could find—and let me tell you; I didn't come home empty-handed. From honey-colored añejos to dark reservas, I hauled bottles back like they were sacred relics. But there was one in particular I just had to buy again: Mamajuana.

For the uninitiated, Mamajuana isn't just a drink, it's an experience. It's a mix of rum, red wine, honey, and a mysterious medley of tree bark, roots, and herbs. Depending on who you ask, it cures the common cold, soothes heartbreak, or turns you into a superhero in the bedroom. Let's just say... I didn't take any chances.

The rum adventure didn't stop there. One of the most unforgettable stops was the Ron Barceló Historical Centre, officially known as Licorería #50. Located on-site at the Ron Barceló distillery, the center is shaped like a barrique (a traditional rum barrel) and offers a full sensory dive into the Dominican Republic's proud rum-making tradition.

Inside, I wandered through exhibits showcasing both cutting-edge distillation and the old-school tools used by early rum masters. The air smelled of sugarcane; the barrels whispered secrets of oak and time, and—yes—there was plenty of tasting.

Among the treasures I brought home were:

+ Ron Barceló Añejo – smooth, deep, and a Dominican classic.

105

- Brugal Doble Reserva – wrapped in its iconic netting, aged in whiskey and sherry casks.
- Bacoo 7-Year-Old Rum – bottled with character and local sugarcane juice.
- Ron Alegro Reserva and XO – rich and elegant expressions of island craftsmanship.
- E. León Jimenes 110 Aniversario – a limited-edition premium rum (No. 1692 of 3000 bottles), bottled in October 2019, crafted in Santiago. This one is special—it was a gift from my son Brandon Peddle, during his trip to the Dominican Republic. And because he's bougie and loves high-end things, of course this was the bottle he had to give me. A premium rum for a premium dad—No. 1692 out of only 3,000 ever made.

I also picked up a stunning red bottle of Machuca, a rum so bold in appearance it practically glows, along with countless memories of sitting by the ocean, glass in hand, bridge stretching out to the water, the sky wide open.

This wasn't just a trip. It was a rum pilgrimage. And somewhere between the Mamajuana and that last glass of Ron Barceló, I found not only some of the best rum in the world—but a renewed appreciation for the stories each bottle carries.

So next time you sip something Dominican, raise a toast to the island's spirit—and maybe, just maybe, your own vitality too.

> A mainlander asked me, 'Is rum part of your culture?'
> I said, "Part? B'y, it's our blood type."

CHAPTER 30

# My Trip to China – Bathroom Shocks and the Search for Rum

China is breathtaking. From the Great Wall to the Forbidden City, it's a country packed with ancient wonders, modern marvels, and more people than you can imagine. But for me, it was also the scene of two great quests:

1. Finding a proper toilet
2. Finding a proper rum

I failed at both. Spectacularly. Yes, they have rum in China—but good luck finding it. It's there, tucked away in places like Yunnan and Guangdong, where a few bold distillers are aging sugarcane spirits that are surprisingly good… if you can track them down. Newfoundland to Chinese was not working for me.

My Newfoundlander accent to the Chinese was something they couldn't understand—or even recognize. To them, I sounded like a pirate who'd just swallowed a mouthful of saltwater and confusion. I asked for directions once, and three people handed me napkins, thinking I was choking. I quickly learned that in China, a smile and hand gestures got me further than words ever could, especially words dipped in cod tongue and George Street slang.

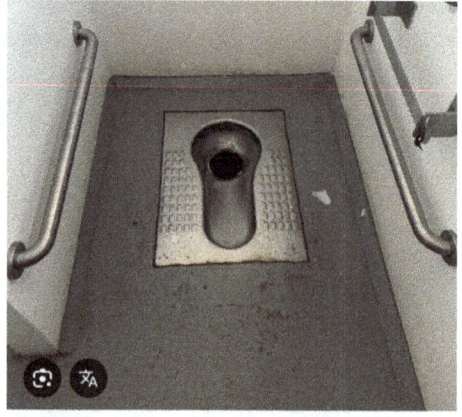

108

## The Sights Were Grand. The Bathrooms Were Not

Let's start with the sightseeing. The Great Wall left me speechless—until I had to go to the bathroom. After hiking for hours, I rushed into a public toilet, expecting something manageable.

Nope.

Just a hole in the floor, two ceramic foot grips, and a paperless future staring back at me. I squatted. I panicked. I nearly tripped.

I gave up. I paid a cab driver $100 USD to get me back to my hotel, and walked out feeling like royalty. Or at least someone with dry shoes.

## The Urinal Gauntlet: A Full-Frontal Cultural Exchange

The next day when I was in China, I figured I'd play it safe with a quick pee while visiting Tiananmen Square. I walked into a public washroom expecting relief — but that's not what I found.

What I got was 50–70 men, pants down to their ankles, shoulder-to-shoulder, at a massive open urinal trough—just letting it fly like it was morning in the rice fields.

The smell could knock a moose down, and I had my T-shirt pulled over my nose, gagging while trying not to make eye contact.

If there was ever a moment I missed Newfoundland, that was it.

## The Search for Rum… and Everything But

Now here's the real kicker.

Being a proud rum lover, I spent the rest of the trip on a mission:

"Do you have any rum?"

Everywhere I went, I asked. Restaurants. Bars. Hotels. Markets. High-end cocktail lounges. The replies came fast—and confusing:

- "No rum, but you want Chinese wine?" (It was warm. And red. And tasted like regret.)
- "Try baijiu!" (China's famous grain liquor—basically lighter fluid in a fancy bottle.)
- "This is rice wine!" (A cloudy potion that made me question my liver's loyalty.)
- "We have whiskey!" (It was Scottish… I cried a little.)
- "How about coconut beer?" (I still don't know what I drank.)

I searched high and low. I would've traded my tour guide for a bottle of Jamaican overproof.

But China wasn't having it.

No rum.

Just confusion, combustion, and cultural enlightenment.

## Final Thoughts from a Rum-Less Travelled

China amazed me. It humbled me.

It also made me realize how deeply attached I am to a good bottle of rum—and modern plumbing.

So if you ever go to China, pack your patience, learn how to hover… and bring your own rum.

You'll thank me later.

**Newfoundland rum motto: If you remember the night, you didn't do it right.**

CHAPTER 31

# The Philippines' Liquid Legend – Tanduay & Tondena Rum

From my global collection, few bottles surprise people more than these: Tanduay and Tondena—proudly Filipino, widely consumed, and quietly dominant on the world stage. In fact, Tanduay has claimed the title of the most-sold rum in the world, beating out even the giants like Bacardi in recent years. You won't always see it on Western shelves, but in Asia and the Pacific, it's everywhere—from street celebrations to high-end bars.

The Philippines has a deep-rooted rum culture shaped by sugarcane, Spanish colonial influence, and tropical heat. Tondena, often called Manila Rum, is another key player—lighter, often gold or clear, and perfectly suited for cocktails or sipping with friends under a swaying palm.

These bottles may not shout from the top shelf, but they represent an entire nation's flavour and pride. And let's be honest—how many people can say they have the world's most-sold rum sitting quietly on their shelf?

Don Papa Rum, distilled on the island of Negros in the Philippines, is as rich in flavour as it is in story. Aged in American oak and named

111

after revolutionary leader Papa Isio, this rum is known for its smooth, dessert-like profile with strong notes of vanilla, orange peel, and caramel. While it's one of the most popular rums in Asia, it's also one of the most debated—thanks to its heavy use of added sugar and flavouring. Love it or leave it, Don Papa is a crowd-pleaser that's earned its spot on the shelf and in many sweet rum cocktails.

> **If you see a Newfoundlander climbing a tree with a bottle of rum—it's not the rum talkin', he's just lookin' for better reception.**

CHAPTER 32

# India – Rum, Spice, and Unexpected Adventures

After China's rum-less rollercoaster, I had high hopes for India. I figured these vibrant, tropical countries—with all their sugarcane, spice, and sunshine—would be rum paradise.

Turns out, it wasn't that simple.

## India: The Land of Curry and Confusion

India was a full-blown sensory overload—in the best way. The colours, the food, the sounds—it hits you all at once. You haven't lived until you've sat in a tuk-tuk going the wrong way down a one-way street while a cow strolls by like it owns the place, during my seven-day adventure, I had curried eggs, curried goat, curried chicken, curried lamb—curried everything. By the end of it, I was sweating turmeric. It was coming out of my pores, like a detox program gone wild.

While in India, I spotted those familiar golden arches—the mighty McDonald's "M"— and I lit up like a fat kid and chocolate cake Visions of Big Macs and Quarter Pounders danced in my head. I got so excited, I ran into the glass door trying to get in.

And that's when the heartbreak began.

It was a meatless McDonald's.

No beef. No bacon. No double cheeseburgers. Just a lineup of unfamiliar names like McAloo Tikki and McVeggie, and a menu that read like a salad bar went to culinary school. Don't get me wrong—the food was fine. But to a Newfoundlander used to gravy-drenched burgers and fish and chips and late-night fries, it felt like I'd walked into a prank show. I ordered something called a Spicy Paneer Wrap, took a bite, and silently paid my respects to the cow that wasn't there.

But I wasn't just there for the food or the sights.

I was on a mission.

"Where can I get some rum?"

The answers varied:

"Rum? We have Old Monk!"

"Rum? Try our whisky, it's better!"

"Rum? We have this... it's kind of rum."

Old Monk turned out to be the local go-to. A dark, syrupy Indian rum that's either legendary or dangerous, depending on who you ask. I gave it a try, and let's just say... it warms more than your throat. It warms your soul. And possibly your organs.

Still, finding a decent pour wasn't easy. Most places pushed Kingfisher beer, feni (a spirit made from cashew fruit), or whisky, which is absolutely everywhere. Rum felt like an afterthought.

But every now and then, a bottle of Old Monk would appear on a dusty shelf like a hidden treasure—and I'd raise a glass like I found the Holy Grail.

During my travels in India, I discovered that the country's love for rum runs just as deep as its love for cricket and curry. The Indian rum scene is bold, spiced, and full of character—just like the people who drink it. As a man who loves curry, I left satisfied. As a man with a limited tolerance for the colour yellow, I left glowing like a lantern. But I wouldn't trade that experience for the world. India gave me flavours to remember, stories to tell, and a whole new appreciation for the fiery romance between curry and rum. Here's a snapshot of the treasures I brought back:

1. Old Monk Gold Reserve 12 Year

- Origin: Mohan Meakin Distillery
- Style: Dark rum, aged 12 years
- Profile: Smooth, rich molasses notes with hints of vanilla and caramel.
- Fun Fact: Once the most popular rum in India—still a cult classic among locals and expats.

2. Amrut Two Indies Rum

- Origin: Amrut Distilleries, Bangalore
- Style: Blend of West Indian and Indian rums
- Profile: Fruity, layered, with both tropical and oak notes.
- Why It Matters: A tribute to the historical triangle of rum—India, the Caribbean, and colonial trade routes.

### 3. Old Monk XXX Rum (Iconic Monk-Shaped Bottle)

- Origin: Mohan Meakin
- Style: Vatted Indian rum
- Icon Alert: The monk-shaped bottle is collectible on its own—known as "Old Monk Legend."

### 4. McDowell's No.1 Celebration Rum

- Origin: United Spirits (a Diageo brand)
- Style: Indian dark rum
- Profile: Lighter than Old Monk, popular across all of India.
- Claim to Fame: One of the world's best-selling rums by volume.

### 5. Amrut Old Port Deluxe Rum

- Origin: Amrut Distilleries
- Style: Traditional Indian dark rum
- Profile: Notes of spice, toffee, and brown sugar.
- Backstory: A favourite for sipping or mixing—smooth and affordable.

### 6. Old Monk Rum Rhum (Short Round Bottle)

- A rare or export-styled edition—bottled for special markets or collectors.
- Dark, velvety, and unmistakably Old Monk in flavor.

> Newfoundlanders don't measure rum in ounces. We use a system called 'Just a Drop'... which is roughly half the bottle.

CHAPTER 33

# Thailand – Rum, Rice, and the Tropical Twist You Didn't See Coming

When you think of Thailand, your mind might go to street food, temples, elephants, or the madness of Bangkok traffic—but rum? That one catches most people off guard. And yet, nestled among palm trees and beach bars, Thailand has been quietly producing some pretty interesting sugarcane spirits.

I made my way to Phuket, on a mission to explore what I called the "Amazing Thailand Rum Trail." This wasn't your average beach vacation—I was on the hunt for every craft of rum I could find, from distillery tastings to local bartender secrets. And what I discovered surprised even a seasoned Rummelier like me.

## A Different Kind of Spirit

Thailand is better known for sangsom, a spirit that many mistake for rum. Technically, it's closer to a molasses-based whisky or neutral spirit infused with caramel—cheap, sweet, and everywhere. It's what the locals mix with cola or Red Bull (and yes, Thai Red Bull is stronger than the stuff we get in the West).

But in recent years, a few dedicated Thai distillers have been pushing for a craft rum revolution—one that's rooted in sugarcane, terroir, and quality over quantity.

## Notable Thai Rums

1. **Chalong Bay Rum (Phuket)**
   This is Thailand's claim to real craft rum fame. Made from fresh-pressed Thai sugarcane juice (not molasses), Chalong Bay is distilled in traditional French copper stills. It's grassy, crisp, and has a distinctly agricole-style character—more like what you'd find in Martinique than the Caribbean party islands.

2. **Phraya Rum**
   Aged in oak barrels near the Mekong River, Phraya is Thailand's premium sipping rum. It's rich, smooth, with notes of spice, honey, and tropical fruit. Marketed as a luxury spirit, it's more likely to be found in upscale lounges than beach bars with hammocks. Of course, I brought home two bottles of each.

## Rum and Thai Culture

Thailand doesn't have the same deep colonial rum roots as the Caribbean, but it has all the right ingredients—literally. Sugarcane grows easily in the country's hot, humid climate, and Thai hospitality means there's no shortage of welcoming bars, inventive cocktails, and smiling strangers willing to share a drink.

And like everything else in Thailand, there's balance. In Buddhist tradition, drinking is done socially, rarely recklessly, and usually paired with food. Even the wildest beach party tends to start with a respectful wai (a small prayer-like bow) and end with pad Thai or a good laugh.

## A Rum Tale from the Road

One night in Krabi, I found myself at a tiny bar made of bamboo and beach dreams. I ordered a "rum cocktail" and watched as the bartender grabbed a dusty bottle, poured a heavy splash into a coconut, and topped it with who-knows-what. It tasted like gasoline and regret—but the sunset, the waves, and the laugh I had with the bartender made it one of the best drinks I've ever had.

He smiled and said, "You drink Thai rum… you stay Thailand long time."

He wasn't wrong—I stayed two weeks longer than planned.

And here's a little tip from a well-travelled Newfie: never drink more than three rums in a Thai bar. After that, what looks like a beautiful woman might just surprise you—and not in the way you're expecting! I'll leave it at that and let your imagination do the rest.

## Final Sip

Thai rum might not (yet) be on the world stage like Jamaica or Barbados, but it's got something those places can't offer: a blend of tropical serenity, bold experimentation, and that unmistakable Thai charm. Whether it's sipping Chalong Bay on a rooftop in Bangkok or grabbing a mystery bottle in Phuket from a roadside stand with a grin that says "you're in for it," rum in Thailand is an experience I'll never forget.

> **Why did the Thai monk refuse the rum?**
> **Because he already reached "high spirits" through meditation!**

CHAPTER 34

# Gosling's Rum: The Grand Plan Gone Wrong

## The Goslings – How a Rum Empire Accidentally Washed Ashore

You want a funny rum story? Let me tell you how the Gosling family ended up in Bermuda—it wasn't a grand plan, it was more like a divine detour with barrels involved.

In 1806, James Gosling, the son of a prosperous English wine and spirits merchant, set sail for America with £10,000 worth of merchandise and dreams of setting up shop in the New World. But after 91 miserable days at sea, their charter ran out of time, the ship ran out of wind, and the crew ran out of patience.

So what did they do?

They docked at the nearest place with rum and sunshine—Bermuda.

Instead of carrying on to Virginia like they originally planned, the Gosling's set up shop right there on Front Street in Hamilton. And lucky for us, they stayed. What started as a detour turned into over two centuries of rum legacy. Today, Gosling's Black Seal Rum is the heart and soul of Bermuda—and the key ingredient in the island's national drink, the Dark 'n Stormy.

The Dark 'n Stormy, a deceptively simple cocktail made with Gosling's Black Seal Rum and spicy ginger beer, is more than just a drink—it's a national treasure. The name comes from a sailor who looked into the swirling glass and said it was "the color of a cloud only a fool or a dead man would sail under." Gosling's even trademarked the cocktail—so legally, if it's not made with Gosling's rum, it's not a Dark 'n Stormy.

The Gosling family didn't just create a rum—they created a brand tied deeply to the identity of Bermuda. Still family-owned seven generations later, the business has grown from a forced landing to a global rum icon. They didn't just ride out the storm—they bottled it.

So, if anyone asks how the Goslings ended up in Bermuda, the answer is simple: bad timing, great rum, and probably a stiff breeze in the wrong direction.

CHAPTER 35

# From Icebergs to Iguanas: How the Rock Powered Belize

## Rum Memories in Belize – Sun, Saddles, and Sips

On a sun-drenched afternoon in Belize, with the temperature dancing around 30°C and the air thick with the scent of salt and promise, I hired a man named Richard and his horse and buggy to tour the town. It wasn't long before I was clopping past schoolchildren in bright uniforms, waving and smiling like I was royalty. We ambled by colorful shops and old colonial homes until we reached a little liquor store tucked behind a row of palms. That's where I spotted my first bottle of Travellers Parrot 3 Barrel Rum. It was only $12 each but the taste and memory were worth a thousand times that. Smooth, mellow, and packed with the warmth

of Belize itself, every sip still takes me back to that golden afternoon with Richard, his faithful horse, and the easy laughter of children in the sun.

After our scenic tour of the island, we decided to cap off the day with something wild: swimming with the sharks at Hol Chan Marine Reserve and Shark Ray Alley, just off Ambergris Caye, Belize. The water was crystal clear, the sun was blazing, and the Caribbean breeze had just the right amount of salt and swagger.

It was a great day—not like the first time I tried this sort of genius move.

That first time? We were down in Mexico, and took a boat from Cancun to Isla Mujeres. Sounds lovely, right? It was… at first. Until I found myself on a 30-minute boat ride in the blistering sun, sweating like a Sunday roast in a church basement. I had four or five rum drinks by then—pure hydration, really—and by the time we pulled up to the dive spot, I was already half cooked.

My son, Brandon Peddle, cool as a cucumber and full of youthful confidence, looked at me and said:

"Let's go swimming with the stingrays and sharks!"

Now, a normal man might hesitate.

But I'm not normal.

I'm from Newfoundland.

So I said:

"Great idea, b'y!"

And off I went—sweaty, sunbaked, slightly rum-marinated—and flopped into the water like a giant piece of chum. I swear the sharks probably rang a dinner bell. The water was murky, things were brushing past me, and for all I knew, I was floating in a salad bowl of stingrays, seaweed, and regret.

It was not a good idea.

Let me say that again for the b'ys in the back:

It was absolutely, positively NOT a good idea.

So years later, when we did it properly in Belize—with clear water, a real guide, and only one civilized drink beforehand—it was like a completely different experience. We glided alongside nurse sharks, tiptoed past stingrays, and admired vibrant coral like we were in a living postcard.

Brandon? Is Still bold and fearless.

Me? A little more sun-smart, a little more sober, and finally aware that sweating out rum on a reef makes you less of a snorkeler… and more of a floating buffet.

## Belize and The Power of Newfoundland

The funny thing about Belize is that almost everyone I met actually knew where Newfoundland was—and not just vaguely. They didn't blink when I mentioned it. Why? Because Fortis, the Newfoundland-based utility giant, owns 67% of Belize's power company.

One guy even said, "Oh yeah, we get NTV news down here sometimes." I nearly dropped my rum punch. Imagine traveling halfway around the world, only to hear someone mention Storm Watch with Eddie Sheerr like it was the Weather Channel.

Turns out, in Belize, Newfoundland isn't "where's that?"—it's "they own the lights!"

Only in a Newfoundlander's life would you find that the first place people recognize your home isn't Boston, London, or Beijing—it's Belize, because of a power bill.

> There's no such thing as 'just one' drink in Newfoundland. That's just the warm-up for the apology tour the next morning.

CHAPTER 36

# The Rum Raid of 1926 – Belize's Bold Rebellion

In 1926, long before Belize gained independence, it was still under British colonial rule—and like much of the Caribbean, rum flowed freely through its streets, docks, and taverns. But that year, colonial authorities, under pressure from British temperance movements and tightening economic controls, decided to crack down on rum production and trade.

They made a big mistake.

Known locally as "The Rum Raid," colonial police and customs agents launched a surprise operation in Belize City. Barrels were seized from distilleries, private homes, and even churches (which often brewed small batches for 'ceremonial' purposes). Within hours, wagons full of confiscated rum rolled down the cobbled streets, headed for destruction. The goal: to dump them in the sea.

But the people had other plans.

Angry citizens began to gather—dockworkers, farmers, rum traders, and even schoolteachers. A group of dockhands intercepted one of the wagons and tipped it over, spilling the precious contents into the street. Legend has it that locals scrambled with cups, pots, and even their hats to save what they could.

A British officer reportedly declared, "These people have rum in their blood and rebellion in their bones!"

The operation backfired so badly that a few colonial officers were quietly reassigned, and the crackdown was largely abandoned. It became a symbol of resistance—how one little island stood up to imperial control, one barrel at a time.

To this day, Belizean rum makers refer to 1926 as "The Year of the Rum."

> They say rum warms the soul. In Newfoundland, it also defrosts your car door in February.

CHAPTER 37

# Rum and Uncle Sam – How the U.S. Government Got Into Booze

You might think the United States government would keep its hands clean when it comes to rum, but the truth is, they've been neck-deep in barrels, taxes, and courtrooms for over a century. From Prohibition-era chases to modern subsidy programs, Uncle Sam has never been far from the spirit world.

## Prohibition and the Rise of Rum Smuggling

During Prohibition (1920–1933), the U.S. government banned the sale and consumption of alcohol—which, predictably, created a booming black market for Caribbean rum. Smugglers ran booze from the Bahamas, Cuba, and Newfoundland's own neighbour, St. Pierre and Miquelon. The Coast Guard waged a sea battle against rum runners while underground bars flourished across the country. It was one of the greatest backfires in government history.

## The Cover-Over Program – Subsidizing Rum

The U.S. collects excise taxes on rum imported into the mainland, even if it's made in U.S. territories like Puerto Rico and the U.S. Virgin Islands. Under the cover-over program, that tax money is returned to the territory where the rum originated. This funneling of hundreds of millions back to rum-producing islands supports infrastructure, jobs, and rum itself. Yes—Uncle Sam literally helps pay for rum production.

## The Sugar Tax and the Roots of Rebellion

Before rum was even smuggled or taxed at the border, it was caught up in one of the earliest American tax scandals—the Sugar Act of 1764. This British law imposed duties on sugar and molasses imported into the American colonies, directly impacting the rum industry, which relied on molasses as its primary ingredient. It helped spark protests and tensions that eventually led to the American Revolution. Rum and taxes go way back—and they've been inseparable ever since.

## Rum and the U.S. Military

American soldiers abroad have often enjoyed rum—especially during the Spanish-American War and World War II. In places like Cuba, Bermuda, and Newfoundland, rum became part of the barracks' experience, sometimes mixed with Coca-Cola or whatever else was on hand. Though not officially rationed like in the British Navy, rum remained a favoured off-duty indulgence for American forces.

## Bacardi, Cuba, and Washington

After the Cuban Revolution, the U.S. government stepped in to protect Bacardi's rights against the Cuban government's seizure of assets. In 1998, a special law—Section 211 of the Omnibus Appropriations Act—was passed to protect Bacardi's claim to the Havana Club trademark. That's right: Congress literally wrote a law to protect a rum label.

## Final Thoughts

Rum has always been more than a drink—it's been a political weapon, a taxable asset, and a symbol of resistance. And when it comes to booze, the U.S. government doesn't just regulate it—they've helped create, protect, and occasionally ruin the market. So next time you pour a glass of rum, tip a bit out for Uncle Sam. He's earned it—kind of.

"Only in America can your rum be taxed, subsidized, outlawed, protected by Congress, and still be considered contraband—sometimes all at once."

A Newfie walks into a liquor store and says…
"I'm not sayin' I'm drinkin' tonight, b'y—
but I didn't wear socks for nothin'."

## CHAPTER 38

# A Shot of Rum with Your Cough Syrup, Prescriptions & Prohibition

Believe it or not, during Prohibition, you could legally buy alcohol at your local drugstore. That's right—while bars were raided and rum-runners were chased by the Coast Guard, your neighborhood pharmacist was pouring more shots than the average speakeasy.

Knocking back a tipple or two wasn't illegal—as long as you did it in your own home. And if you had the right "medical condition" (which, let's face it, most people suddenly developed), you could get a prescription for rum. Migraines? Rum. Back pain? Rum. Marriage problems? Probably rum, too.

Doctors became part-time bartenders, and pharmacies turned into classy watering holes with medicine cabinets full of booze-in-disguise. All it took was a cooperative doctor, a few bucks, and a wink.

And just like that, the American public got a taste of what it meant to drink responsibly—for medical purposes only, of course.

Doctor told me to take two shots and call him in the morning. So I took four and didn't call anyone.

They said it was for "medicinal use only," so I kept my bottle in the first aid kit—right next to the Band-Aids and the holy water.

My buddy said he had a cold, so I poured him a double. He hasn't coughed since—though he also hasn't stood up straight either.

> Screeched-in last night. Kissed the cod, said the oath, drank the rum. Still single. Guess the cod has high standards.

CHAPTER 39

# Rum in the White House – President Harding's Wet Cabinet

While the rest of the U.S. was forced to go dry under the Volstead Act, one man made sure the White House bar stayed very wet: President Warren G. Harding.

Elected in 1920, just as Prohibition was kicking off, Harding publicly supported the 18th Amendment—but behind closed doors, he was throwing poker nights that would make a pirate blush. In fact, his inner circle became known as the "Ohio Gang," a collection of advisors and friends known for bribery, scandal—and their love of fine drink, especially Caribbean rum.

Harding had rum smuggled in through private channels. Some came by train from Cuba, others were sourced from diplomatic shipments. His butler reportedly kept a special cabinet just for his rum collection, featuring bottles from Barbados, Puerto Rico, and Trinidad.

One night, during a heated poker game, Harding is said to have raised a glass of Barbados rum and joked:

"I may be the Commander-in-Chief, but I take orders from this little bottle."

While the country struggled with bootleggers, speakeasies, and raids, the White House remained a safe haven for rum and other spirits. Harding's hypocrisy wasn't lost on the public once the stories leaked—but oddly enough, it only made him more popular with everyday Americans who were tired of the dry laws.

Harding died suddenly in 1923 during a trip to San Francisco, and though the cause was officially a heart attack, conspiracy theories still swirl—some claiming he was poisoned by his wife, others suggesting years of hard drinking caught up with him.

But one thing is certain: Prohibition never made it to 1600 Pennsylvania Avenue.

> A mainlander asked if screech tastes good.
> I said, 'After the first shot, it don't matter.

CHAPTER 40

# NASCAR & Rumrunners – From Booze to Burnouts

When you think of NASCAR, you might picture roaring engines, southern grandstands, and high-octane sponsors. But peel back the asphalt history, and you'll find its roots soaked in moonshine and rum.

During Prohibition in the United States (1920–1933), the liquor business didn't dry up—it went underground. Bootleggers and rum runners were in high gear, smuggling alcohol from the Caribbean, Canada, and backwoods stills into the thirsty towns and cities of America. And to stay ahead of the law, they had to drive fast—very fast.

To outrun federal agents, these bootleggers began modifying their cars. They would soup up the engines, reinforce the suspensions, and tweak the bodies to make them look like ordinary family sedans—until they hit the gas. These were the original getaway cars, often loaded with hidden compartments filled with rum, whiskey, or moonshine.

By the late 1930s, the "rumrunners" and "shine haulers" started racing each other for bragging rights on weekends, especially down south. That rebellious spirit, combined with the love of speed, eventually evolved into stock car racing. By 1948, NASCAR (the National Association for Stock Car Auto Racing) was officially born.

Many of NASCAR's early heroes—like Junior Johnson, whose family ran moonshine—learned to drive on dusty back roads with a trunk full of illegal liquor and a federal agent in the rearview mirror.

So the next time you hear engines rev at Daytona or Talladega, remember: the thunder of those tires was born from the need to deliver rum, not trophies. In fact, you could say that every left turn in NASCAR is a toast to its rum-running past.

**What's the difference between a NASCAR driver and a Newfoundlander during a rum shortage?**
One goes in circles real fast, the other will circle the bay until he finds a bottle.

CHAPTER 41

# Spirits, Superstitions & the Rum That Sees All

Wherever rum flows, so do the stories—and in many places around the world, those stories lean toward the supernatural. From haunted distilleries in the Caribbean to sailor's omens and ghostly figures glimpsed at sea, rum and spirits—both kinds—are forever intertwined.

In the West Indies, it's believed that certain rums should never be poured without first giving a little offering to the ancestors. Some islanders will pour a splash on the ground, saying "for the spirits," before they even raise their glass. And don't even think about toasting without making eye contact—it's said to bring seven years of bad luck… and terrible hangovers.

In Haiti and parts of the Dominican Republic, rum is central to Vodou ceremonies, offered to the lwa (spirits) to invite blessings—or sometimes protection—from forces beyond this world. In fact, if a bottle mysteriously empties overnight, locals might simply shrug and say, "The spirits were thirsty."

Even among sailors, rum had its superstitions. Spilling your tot was a bad omen. Drinking with your left hand invited Poseidon's wrath, and a cork that popped on its own was believed to mean a ghost was near—or someone was about to get very drunk.

And let's not forget Newfoundland, where every bottle of rum comes with a bit of a wink and a warning. Whether it's Old Sam whispering secrets or Screech bottling a banshee, we always say: If your rum bottle starts moving on its own—either you've had too much, or you've just invited a P.E.I. poltergeist.

## Rum in Literature and Legends – From Twain to Pirates

Rum isn't just a drink—it's a character in stories, a muse for writers, and the heartbeat of sea-soaked legends. From the smoky backrooms of colonial taverns to the pages of classic novels, rum has left ink stains on the hands of some of the world's greatest storytellers.

Mark Twain, who loved to drink almost as much as he loved to write, often found inspiration at the bottom of a glass. While not always naming rum directly, he once remarked, "Too much of anything is bad, but too much good whiskey is barely enough." We know he meant rum too—after all, he traveled to the Caribbean and Hawaii, where sugarcane spirits flowed freely.

Why don't Newfoundlanders ever drink rum under a full moon?
Because last time they did, Uncle Barry started howling,
took off his pants, and swore he saw a ghost named "Marg."
Turns out it was just the neighbour's laundry.

CHAPTER 42

# The West Indies Rum Syndicate – Caribbean Cartels

While America was busy banning booze, the Caribbean saw a golden opportunity. Rum demand skyrocketed—especially from the United States—and island producers stepped up. But behind the cheerful labels and tropical brands, there was a secretive alliance pulling the strings.

## Welcome to the West Indies Rum Syndicate.

In the early 1920s, major rum-producing islands like Barbados, Jamaica, Trinidad, and the Virgin Islands quietly formed a cooperative network. Their goal? To control prices, limit overproduction, and secretly coordinate smuggling routes into the thirsty United States. Though never officially documented (because you don't leave a paper trail when you're evading the U.S. Coast Guard), distillers often met under the guise of trade talks and tourism conferences.

They set minimum prices for rum barrels, agreed not to flood the market, and used legitimate shipping manifests to hide casks of high-proof gold and dark rum bound for Florida, New York, and even Boston.

One famous story tells of a Jamaican distiller who marked his rum barrels as "fish sauce" and shipped them to a Boston seafood company—with instructions to "serve chilled." Another tale tells of casks hidden in banana shipments, guarded by dockworkers paid in sips and cigars.

It worked. Rum from the Caribbean became the drink of choice for Prohibition-era parties and speakeasies. The Syndicate's rum was smooth, aged, and far safer than the dangerous moonshine being brewed in American bathtubs.

Some say the Syndicate's success funded beautiful homes, better schools, and even the first radio station in Barbados. Others say it helped fund pirate-like fortunes for a few well-connected families.

Either way, the Caribbean didn't just survive Prohibition—they thrived on it.

---

**What did the drunk pirate say at the job interview?**
"I'm a little overqualified... I've got 30 years of rum experience and a parrot for HR."

CHAPTER 43

# Bathtub Rum – America's Homebrew Havoc

When Prohibition hit in 1920, Americans didn't just stop drinking—they got creative. While "bathtub gin" became the poster child of the era, rum had its own wild underground moment. And trust me, it wasn't pretty.

Desperate to replicate the Caribbean's favourite spirit, amateur chemists from Boston to Boise began brewing "bathtub rum". The basic idea? Mix industrial alcohol (often meant for paint thinner or cleaning supplies) with water, molasses, sugar, and a splash of spice... then let it sit in the tub.

Literally. In the tub.

The problem? Industrial alcohol was often poisonous. To avoid detection, the U.S. government had even intentionally poisoned alcohol supplies with methanol and other toxins. Thousands died or went blind trying to drink this homemade hooch. But that didn't stop the "bathtub barons" who charged a top dollar for what they called "Navy-style rum." Most of it tasted like cough syrup and regret.

In Chicago, one infamous bootlegger named "Rummy Joe" even added vanilla extract, prune juice, and axle grease to his recipe. Locals swore it made you hallucinate sea shanties and talk like a pirate for a week.

Still, the thirst for rum was real—and some batches actually came out half-decent. A few smart bootleggers began importing small bottles of real Caribbean rum and diluting it with molasses and grain alcohol to stretch profits.

Others just gave up and started smuggling again.

Bathtub rum faded away after Prohibition ended in 1933, but the legacy lives on in cocktail culture—and in the lesson that not everything made in your bathroom should be consumed.

> **Doctor told me to cut down on rum.**
> **So now I only drink it from short glasses.**

CHAPTER 44

# Rum Running by Sea Plane – Sky Smugglers of Prohibition

While most rum runners stuck to boats and back roads, a few bold pioneers looked to the skies—and found a new frontier for smuggling. Enter the sea plane rum runners of the 1920s and '30s.

As the Coast Guard tightened its grip on the shoreline, clever smugglers began using sea planes to leapfrog over patrols and deliver rum directly to secluded beaches, swampy inlets, and even rooftop drop-offs. These weren't your average pilots—they were ex-World War I flyboys, daredevils with nerves of steel, and a taste for danger (and dark rum).

One of the most legendary was a man known only as "Captain Midnight." Based out of the Florida Keys, he operated a rickety Curtis seaplane, loading it up in Havana with Cuban rum—often stacked to the cockpit. He'd fly at dusk or just before dawn, hugging the waves and dodging patrols, before making daring landings in the Everglades or behind secret speakeasies in Miami.

Locals would run out with flashlights or burning torches in hand to guide him in—like modern-day pirates using runway lights made of moonlight and guts.

Sea plane smuggling became so common that Florida authorities were forced to station lookouts on rooftops, armed with binoculars. But the skies were hard to police, and rum kept flowing like the tides.

Some smugglers even painted their planes with fake U.S. Postal Service logos, giving them free rein to land just about anywhere.

By the end of Prohibition, sea plane rum running was less common—but not before leaving a legend in its wake. Today, a few old-timers in the Keys still say, "You can't hear a buzzin' plane at sunset without smellin' molasses."

> They asked if I wanted my rum on the rocks. I said no thanks—I already fell on the ice once today.

CHAPTER 45

# Rum Runners' Row – New Jersey's Boozy Shoreline

During Prohibition, the New Jersey coastline became one of the most notorious smuggling hotspots in North America. They called it "Rum Runners' Row," and from Sandy Hook to Cape May, every inlet, wharf, and fishing boat was part of a massive underground operation.

Just three miles off the coast was the key: international waters. Beyond that invisible line, the U.S. had no legal jurisdiction. So a floating armada of ships—called "Rum Row"—would anchor just outside the limit, loaded with Caribbean rum, Canadian whisky, and even French champagne.

These ships operated like offshore liquor stores, selling their wares to smaller speedboats that zipped back and forth to shore under the cover of darkness.

New Jersey's organized crime families got in on the action fast. Atlantic City, in particular, became the crown jewel of the coast. Under the corrupt but charming political boss Enoch "Nucky" Johnson (yes, the real-life inspiration for Boardwalk Empire), the city openly welcomed rum runners. Speakeasies flourished, and waiters offered you "fish or fowl—or the good stuff."

Locals joined in, too. Lobstermen pulled up traps and returned with crates of Jamaican overproof. Housewives baked pies with "a secret filling" straight from Havana. Even some Coast Guard officers were caught looking the other way—for a small share of the cargo.

One famous runner, "Speedboat Charlie," was known to hit 60 mph on the open sea in his custom-built vessel. He'd deliver six cases at a time and never once got caught—thanks to bribes, back alleys, and a few well-placed foghorn signals.

By the end of Prohibition, Rum Runners' Row had become a legend. And to this day, old timers in Atlantic City still say,

"If those dunes could talk, they'd be drunk."

**Brought a bottle of rum to Nan's house. She said, "Put it next to the holy water. We'll bless it later."**

CHAPTER 46

# The French Foreign Legion and Liquid Courage

Few outfits in military history carry as much mystique as the French Foreign Legion—a force of outcasts, adventurers, and lost souls who served in some of the harshest places on Earth. But behind their fearsome reputation was a daily ritual of survival, and it came in the form of one thing: rum.

Stationed in the blistering deserts of North Africa, legionnaires endured unbearable heat, sandstorms, and brutal training. To keep morale high (and tempers low), French commanders issued daily rations of rum, often mixed with water—or, in some cases, straight up poured into their canteens.

The rum was usually strong, dark, and packed a punch. Some called it "le feu liquide"—liquid fire. But the men came to depend on it. It dulled the pain, soothed nerves, and made their isolation a bit more bearable.

It also gave rise to wild rituals. Every evening, after inspection, legionnaires would form circles to share their rum, tell stories of past battles, or sing drunken songs in French, Spanish, German, and even Russian. One of the more famous sayings of the time was:

"March or die—but drink before both."

There are even records of entire skirmishes won by sheer audacity, where half-drunk units stormed hills shouting, "Pour la bouteille!"

The Legion's rum rations became so embedded in their identity that when the French military tried to cut supplies during WWII, it triggered protests—and even a brief mutiny in Morocco.

Today, while the modern Legion no longer relies on rum, veterans still gather annually to toast with a shot of the old stuff. They raise their glasses high and remember the days when the sun was cruel; the battles were long, and the rum was always strong.

> **Only in Newfoundland will someone offer you a cure for a cold, a heartbreak, and a moose bite—and it's the same bottle of rum every time.**

CHAPTER 47

# Fake Lighthouses and Florida Keys' Rum Havens

During Prohibition, the Florida Keys weren't just a tropical escape—they were a smugglers' paradise. With over 800 islands, countless hidden coves, and a laid-back culture that didn't take kindly to federal rules, it became one of the hottest rum-running routes in the Americas.

But what made it truly legendary was a trick straight out of a pirate's playbook: fake lighthouses.

Local rum runners—and yes, even a few retired fishermen—would rig up fake light signals along the coast using lanterns, mirrors, and rotating tin cans. To the untrained eye, these flickers looked just like official navigation beacons guiding incoming boats. But instead of leading ships to safety, they guided rum-laden schooners and speedboats into secret inlets where barrels were offloaded, buried in the sand, or hidden in crab shacks.

Some Keys residents even built entire decoy docks, complete with fake Coast Guard flags to trick nosey authorities. Others took it a step further—disguising their boats as shrimping vessels, complete with nets and fake catches piled over crates of Jamaican and Cuban rum.

And the local law? Let's just say it had a very "live and let drink" approach.

One of the most famous tales involves a Key West bartender named "Salty Sam," who ran a beachfront bar with a trapdoor under the barstool. Every night, Sam would lower fresh cases of rum from Havana down into the sand before the feds made their routine rounds. When asked what was under the floor, Sam reportedly said,

"Just some old roots… and the truth."

The Keys didn't just import rum—they celebrated it. Entire beach parties were thrown in honour of new shipments. And the locals didn't see themselves as criminals—they saw themselves as patriots resisting a joyless law.

Today, many of the old smugglers' routes are snorkeling sites and kayak trails. But if you look closely at the right time of night, some locals swear you can still see a flicker in the distance—a rogue beacon calling one last rum boat home.

> **A Newfie walks into a liquor store and says…**
> **"I'm not sayin' I'm drinkin' tonight, b'y—**
> **but I didn't wear socks for nothin'."**

CHAPTER 48

# Puerto Rico's Sugar Wars and Tax Rebellions

Puerto Rico has long been a powerhouse of rum production. Brands like Don Q, Ron del Barrilito, and later Bacardi (after fleeing Cuba) made the island a central figure in the global rum trade. But during and after Prohibition, rum wasn't just a drink—it was the heart of an all-out economic rebellion known as the Sugar Wars.

At the time, the U.S. government implemented something called the "cover-over program"—a policy that allowed excise taxes collected on Puerto Rican rum sold on the mainland to be sent back to Puerto Rico. Sounds helpful, right?

Well, it was... until the Feds started changing the rules.

Small, family-owned Puerto Rican rum distilleries began getting squeezed by U.S. tax law, corporate pressure, and shady government deals that favoured the big players. To make things worse, some island distilleries were accused of "falsifying" records to get around production limits and tax quotas.

In response, local workers, farmers, and independent distillers organized protests—some peaceful, others not. Molotov cocktails were thrown during one fiery demonstration in Ponce in the 1930s, and sugar plantations went up in flames as labourers demanded fair treatment and the freedom to brew and export their own rum.

This wasn't just about taxes—it was about identity. For many Puerto Ricans, rum was more than a product. It was culture. It was pride. It was independence in a bottle.

Eventually, after years of negotiation and activism, new agreements were reached that allowed the island's rum producers to flourish again. But the bitterness over those "sugar wars" still lingers today, especially among the older generation who remember when a bottle of rum could spark a revolution.

And if you ever visit a family distillery in Puerto Rico, they'll raise a glass and say,

"Esto no es solo ron… es resistencia."

(This is not just rum… it's resistance.)

> Sailors used to mix rum and gunpowder to prove its strength. I just mix mine with regret.

CHAPTER 49

# Puerto Rican Rums: The Powerhouse of the Caribbean… Without a Vote

Puerto Rico is one of the largest rum producers in the world—over 70% of the rum consumed in the United States comes from this island. Yet, despite being a U.S. territory since 1898, Puerto Ricans still cannot vote for the President of the United States. They send soldiers to American wars, pay into federal programs, and—yes—drink and distill the very rum that fuels a nation's cocktails, but their political voice in Washington is limited.

I remember sitting down with a local bartender just outside of San Juan. Between pours of Don Q and Bacardí, he said, "We give America rum, music, and baseball legends—and still, we have no vote." That hit me like a splash of overproof.

## Bacardí

- The most internationally known brand—originally from Cuba, now headquartered in Puerto Rico after the Cuban Revolution.
- Light, clean rums aged in charred American oak and charcoal-filtered.
- Perfect for Mojitos, Cuba Libres, or just poured over ice in the Caribbean sun.

## Don Q (Destilería Serrallés)

- The local champion—often more loved than Bacardí on the island.
- Family-owned since 1865, one of the oldest rum-producing families in the Caribbean.
- Highlights include:
- Don Q Cristal – crisp, clean white rum for mixing.
- Don Q Añejo – golden, smooth, and great on the rocks.
- Don Q Gran Reserva XO – aged elegance with depth and character.
- Their distillery is zero-waste, making it one of the most environmentally conscious in the world.

## Rum, Revenue, and the "Cover-Over"

The U.S. government provides a cover-over subsidy: federal excise taxes collected from rum sold in the U.S. are returned to Puerto Rico and the U.S. Virgin Islands. This has made rum production a lifeline for the island's economy. But it's a strange relationship—Puerto Ricans contribute economically and culturally, yet still lack the fundamental right to vote federally.

> "If you can distill it, age it, bottle it, and export it—surely you've earned the right to vote on who runs the place you're sending it to."

CHAPTER 50

# Harlem Renaissance and Rum's Jazz Legacy

When you think of the Harlem Renaissance, you think of art, music, and poetry exploding with rhythm and soul. But behind the saxophones, smoky clubs, and spoken word brilliance, there was something else flowing just as smoothly: rum.

In the 1920s, Harlem was the heartbeat of African American culture—a haven for artists, writers, and musicians pushing boundaries. And like every great cultural movement, it needed a spark... and maybe a splash of something strong. That's where Caribbean rum came in.

Caribbean immigrants, especially from the West Indies, brought their traditions, music, and rum with them. Small shops in Harlem quietly sold Jamaican overproof, Trinidadian dark rum, and home-brewed concoctions straight from Brooklyn basements. Some bottles were smuggled through Havana, others came in on banana boats disguised as tropical exports.

The speakeasies of Harlem were legendary: The Cotton Club, The Savoy Ballroom, Small's Paradise—places where Duke Ellington played piano, Billie Holiday sang the blues, and Langston Hughes wrote poetry that felt like thunder.

And while bootleg whiskey was common downtown, Harlem had its own signature drink: the Rum Punch. Strong, spiced, and sweet, it became the unofficial cocktail of Harlem nights. One jazz player famously said,

"Play me a solo, pour me a rum, and let me feel free."

Rum wasn't just a drink—it was a cultural bridge. It connected Harlem to Havana, Kingston, Port of Spain, and beyond. It was present at art shows, in jazz clubs, at late-night domino games, and in the hands of visionaries who refused to be silenced.

And even as Prohibition agents tried to raid the clubs, Harlem found a way to keep the party going. The music wouldn't stop. The poetry wouldn't fade. And the rum kept pouring.

Because sometimes, freedom comes in four-four time—and is served over ice.

> Why did the Newfoundlander pour rum on his lawn mower?
> Because it wasn't cutting it—and he figured it needed a boost.

CHAPTER 51

# I Drink Rum to Save the Planet (You're Welcome)

## A Newfoundlander's Guide to Guilt-Free Sippin', Tree-Huggin', and Proper Educatin'

Let me start by saying something important:

"I'm not just drinking rum... I'm doing my part to save the world."

That's right. As a proud Newfoundlander—raised between salt air and stronger spirits—this Chapter is about how I'm helping the environment one pour at a time, and educating people about it too. And yes, I'm doing it all from my seat at the bar.

You think the mainland crowd is shocked when they hear we get snow in June? Wait till they hear some of the best rums in the world are green—and I don't mean with food coloring on St. Paddy's Day.

## Welcome to the World of Eco-Rums

These are not just bottles; they're acts of environmental heroism. Somewhere between the sugarcane fields and the stills, these distilleries figured out how to save the planet—and keep your glass full.

Here's a breakdown of the finest planet-saving rums I've ever had the honour of sampling (for science, of course):

## Don Q – Puerto Rico's Zero-Waste Wonder

- Turns waste into biogas, recycles every drop of water, and composts leftovers.
- Basically the Ron MacLean of rum: clean, classy, and holding it all together.

## Flor de Caña – Nicaragua's Fair-Trade Favourite

- Carbon-neutral, fair-trade certified, and they plant more trees than I have old fishing gear in the shed.
- Drinking this is like recycling… but with better stories.

# Mount Gay – Barbados' Solar-Powered Legend

- Recycles water, uses solar panels, and is older than some of the jokes that get told at the legion.
- This isn't just good rum—it's guilt-free rum.

# Renegade Rum – Grenada's Green Beast

- Organic farming, rainwater harvesting, and traceability down to the sugarcane's middle name.
- These lads are serious, but the rum still goes down easy.

# Neisson Rhum Agricole – Moon-Farmed Magic from Martinique

- Biodynamic rum made under moonlight and good vibes.
- One glass and you're somewhere between spiritual awakening and island karaoke.

# Montanya Distillers – Colorado's High-Altitude Do-Gooders

- Female-owned, wind-powered, and B Corp certified.
- If Mother Nature ran a distillery, it'd look like this—just with more flannel.

# PART IV

# Newfoundland's Rum Legacy

CHAPTER 52

# The Rums of Newfoundland – Heritage in Every Bottle

Newfoundland's relationship with rum isn't just cultural—it's carved into our identity. From sea-worn schooners trading cod for casks, to kitchen tables where nan kept the bottle behind the tea tins, rum in Newfoundland is about history, humour, and home.

Whether it's the deep molasses warmth of Old Sam, the rowdy party spirit of George Street Spiced, or the wild crafted brilliance of Gunpowder and Rose, every bottle tells a story.

## Classic Newfoundland Rums

### 1. Screech Rum

The undisputed icon. Originally overproof Jamaican rum brought in through trading ports like St. John's, Screech earned its name from the reaction it caused. It became famous for its role in the Screech-In ceremony, where visitors kiss a cod and become honorary Newfoundlanders. Today's Screech is smoother—but no less legendary.

Screech Rum. #1 Selling dark rum in Newfoundland and enjoyed from coast to coast in Canada.

Screech Honey Flavoured Rum

A smooth, sweet twist on Newfoundland's iconic rum. This honey-infused version blends Jamaican rum at 35% ABV with natural honey flavours, bringing in notes of citrus, vanilla, oak, and spice.

It's mellow, easy to sip, and perfect for folks who want a softer Screech experience—with no added sugar and a warm honey finish that pairs beautifully with tea, cocktails, or even over ice cream.

ABV: 35% | 375ml

## 2. Old Sam Rum

A true old-school staple. Dark, molasses-rich, and beloved by generations who kept it close through storms, snow, and Sunday suppers. It's strong enough to warm your chest and your memories.

## 3. Ragged Rock Rum

A newer offering from the NLC that paid tribute to Newfoundland's rugged beauty. Smooth, affordable, and gone too soon—but fondly remembered by those who grabbed a bottle while they could.

## 4. George Street Spiced Rum

A sweet, cinnamon-forward party rum that captured the nightlife spirit of St. John's most famous street. Limited edition but full of fun—just like the street it celebrates.

## 5. Iceberg Rum

Made with water from real North Atlantic icebergs. Clean, bright, and distinctly Newfoundland in both story and purity. An exciting modern take that hints at the future of our island's distilling.

# Modern Newfoundland Rums

### 6. HMSC St. John's Rum

Bottled at 100 proof (57.1%), this rum was created to honour the HMCS St. John's naval vessel. Bold, red-labeled, and made by Favell's, this is a collector's favourite and a salute to our island's military ties.

### 7. Hibernia Ultra Premium Rum

A 5-year-old sipping rum rooted in Irish-Newfoundland tradition. Luxuriously smooth with deep character, this bottle belongs on the top shelf—and often comes out for toasts to family, heritage, and hard-earned victories.

### 8. Newfoundlander's White Rum Collection

This clean, cocktail-ready white rum is packaged in distinctive square bottles with artwork honouring Newfoundland's maritime and trade history. One label proudly states:

"For over a century, our fishing fleets travelled to the Caribbean to trade their precious catch for delectable rums and sugars… a continued tradition in which we take great pride."

It's not just rum—it's a reflection of who we are and where we've been.

### 9. Big Dipper Rum

With a name like Big Dipper, this rum was meant to guide Newfoundlanders through any kind of weather—foggy nights, hard times, or just a long kitchen party. Available in both Light and Dark versions, it was the kind of bottle that showed up at weddings, wakes, and everything in between.

## 10. Cabot Tower Rhum

Named after the iconic signal tower overlooking St. John's, Cabot Tower Rhum stood tall as a bold and distinguished local spirit. It had a label as rugged as the cliffs of Signal Hill, and a taste just as strong.

> "You can judge a Newfoundland rum by its burn, its label—or whether Nan would let you hide it behind the tea tins."

CHAPTER 53

# Made on the Rock – The Rums of Newfoundland & the Screech-In Tradition

Over the years, Newfoundland Screech Rum has undergone several label transformations, each reflecting the brand's evolving identity while maintaining its deep-rooted connection to Newfoundland's culture and heritage.

## A Brief History of Screech Rum

Originally, the rum that would become known as Screech was a high-strength Jamaican rum, a staple in Newfoundland due to trade between Newfoundland and the West Indies. In the early 20th century, when the Newfoundland government took control of alcohol distribution, this rum was sold in unlabelled bottles. The name "Screech" emerged during World War II, inspired by the reaction of American servicemen to the potent drink.

# Evolution of Screech Rum Labels

## 1. Unlabelled Beginnings (Early 20th Century)

In its earliest days under government control, Screech was sold in plain bottles without labels, focusing solely on the rum's potency rather than branding.

## 2. Introduction of the "Screech" Name (Post-WWII)

Following the anecdote involving American servicemen, the Newfoundland Liquor Corporation began officially branding the rum as "Screech," introducing labels that highlighted its Jamaican origins and Newfoundland bottling.

## 3. Colorful Cartographic Labels (Late 20th Century)

Later labels featured vibrant colors, including yellow, blue, and gold, and depicted maps of Newfoundland, emphasizing the rum's local significance.

## 4. Nautical and Vintage Aesthetic (2004 Redesign)

In 2004, Screech underwent a significant label redesign to appeal to a broader market. The new label featured an aged parchment look, a compass rose, and maritime imagery, aligning with Newfoundland's seafaring heritage.

## 5. Modern Minimalist Design (Recent Years)

The most recent labels have adopted a cleaner, more minimalist design, focusing on the brand name and subtle nautical elements, reflecting contemporary branding trends while maintaining a connection to its roots.

## Visual Journey of Screech Labels

To fully appreciate the evolution of Screech Rum's labels, consider exploring the following images:

- Early Colorful Label: Featuring vibrant colors and a map of Newfoundland.
- 2004 Redesign: Showcasing the aged parchment look with nautical themes.
- Modern Label: A minimalist design with subtle maritime elements.

The transformation of Screech Rum's labels over the years reflects a balance between honoring Newfoundland's rich cultural heritage and adapting to modern branding aesthetics. Each label tells a story, capturing the spirit of the island and its people.

# Screech-Ins, Saltwater, and My Mother Patricia

You can't talk about rum in Newfoundland without tipping your hat—and your bottle—to Screech. And you definitely can't talk about Screech without diving headfirst into the most sacred ceremony of all: the Screech-In.

For over 20 years now, I've had the honour (and hilarity) of hosting Screech-Ins across the island, from backyard family BBQs to full-blown performances at The Wilds Golf Course, where guests have flown in from every corner of the globe—including as far as Australia. They don't leave the same.

It's not just a quick kiss-the-cod-and-go kind of thing with me. I go full out—dressed like an old native Newfoundland salt, beard and all. We haul out the rubber boots, oilskins, Sou'wester hats, and get everyone dressed up in full fishing regalia. I make them earn it.

# Hearts Content Newfoundland Screech-In

We start with food, of course—cod tongues (fried crispy), fresh raisin bread with partridgeberry jam, and the real gut-check: a cod liver oil capsule, which I jokingly call "Newfie Viagra." Gets a laugh every time, even if their stomachs don't always agree.

Then we dance. Oh yes, they've got to jig. We belt out a Newfoundland song, usually off-key and full of heart. After that, I have them step into salt water—actual ocean water I've lugged in just for the occasion—and I baptize them right there in the name of wind, waves, and salt cod.

Only then do they take the sacred swig of Screech, pucker up and kiss the cod (real or rubber depending on how fresh we are that day), and sing the Ode to Newfoundland like they were born and raised in Heart's Content.

At the end, I hand out certificates. Some come stamped from the Newfoundland Liquor Commission, others are cheeky versions

Patricia Peddle Doing screech-In's ( yes the one with the beard )

I've made myself—proof that these brave souls are now Honourary Newfoundlanders.

## Patricia Peddle

You Have to have your feet in the Atlantic Ocean to do it Properly

And behind all of it, whether I'm up in Fort McMurray or down on the rocky shores of Conception Bay, I carry with me the spirit of my mother, Patricia Peddle of Heart's Content, who gave me the love of this place, its people, and our way of celebrating. Her legacy lives in every Screech-In, every cod tongue, and every laugh.

Because being a Newfoundlander isn't just about geography—it's about heart, humour, and a little rum.

## 1. Screech Rum: The Legend That Made You Holler

Imported from Jamaica, bottled in Newfoundland, and infused with local legend, Screech got its name when American soldiers stationed here during WWII were offered a drink by a local. The rum was so strong, the poor Yank let out a scream so loud, the whole outport turned around.

The Newfoundlander calmly said,

"It's just the screech, b'y."

And a legend was born.

It was overproof back then—rocket fuel with molasses. Today's version is smoother, aged, and perfect for ceremonies, parties, and making friends question their life choices.

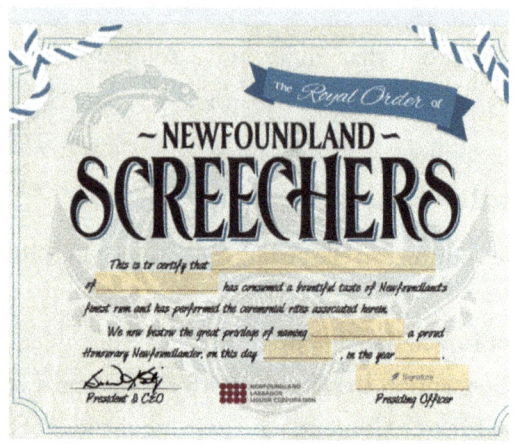

## 2. The Screech-In Ceremony – What It Is, Where to Go, and What to Say

If you've never been screeched in, you're missing out.

Here's how it goes…

WHERE CAN YOU GET SCREECHED IN?

- Christian's Pub – George Street, St. John's (The most famous)
- O'Reilly's Irish Pub – Also on George Street, with a side of live music
- Private Cabins and Kitchens – Pretty much anywhere there's rum and a Newfoundlander with a loud voice
- Tour Boats and Heritage Nights – Especially in outport towns where humour flows freer than electricity

THE CEREMONY:

1. Get a shot of Screech.
   No substitutions. (Don't ask for dark rum or rum cream—we'll laugh.)
2. Kiss the cod.
   Yes, a real (usually frozen) Atlantic codfish. Bonus points if it still smells like the wharf.
   It's more disturbing than romantic, but hey—it's tradition.

3. Repeat the Oath:
   Loud and proud, usually coached by a Newfoundlander half in the bag:
   "Long may yer big jib draw!"
   (Translation: May the wind always be at your back.)
4. Down the Screech.
   All of it. No sippin'. No sniffin'. Just tip 'er back, b'y.
5. You are now an honorary Newfoundlander.
   You may now complain about weather, brag about the fish you caught, and use the word "b'y" in any sentence without judgment.

## Funny Moments from Screech-Ins

- One American tourist kissed the wrong end of the cod.
  Nobody corrected him. It's still talked about.
- A stag party in Corner Brook got screeched in and then lost the groom.
  He turned up in Gander with a "Screech Made Me Do It" tattoo.
- A woman from Germany did the shot, kissed the cod, and proposed to the guy next to her.
  (He accepted. They're still married—sort of.)

### Bonus Joke

"Do I have to kiss the cod?"

*Only if you want to stay.*

## Full Screech-In Script (Use This at Home or Abroad!)

Leader: "Are ye a screecher?"

Group: "Indeed I is, me ol' cock! And long may yer big jib draw!"

Leader: "Kiss the cod!" (Hold the fish like it's royalty. Lip contact is mandatory.)

Leader: "Now slam that shot of Screech and make it look like ya enjoy it!"

### Final Toast

Screech may not be the fanciest rum.

It may not win gold in Paris or silver in San Francisco.

They say the closer you get to sea level, the better the distillation process.

> What's the difference between a screech-in and a wedding?
> Not much—there's kissing a fish, dancing on tables, and someone always forgets what happened the next morning

CHAPTER 54

# Newfoundland Distillery in Clarke Beach

## The Newfoundland Distillery Co. – Rum from the Rock

Heart's Content in Trinity Bay is just 40 minutes from The Newfoundland Distillery in Conception Bay, a gem in the world of craft spirits—and a rising star in Canadian rum. Founded in 2016 in Clarke's Beach, this distillery proudly crafts its rum with the same care and character that defines Newfoundland itself.

What sets their rum apart? For starters, it's made right at sea level, where distillers believe the atmospheric pressure contributes to a smoother, cleaner spirit. The distillery uses locally grown ingredients and infuses their rums with distinct maritime influences—from the salt air to hand-picked botanicals.

One standout creation is their Gunpowder and Rose Rum—a uniquely Newfoundland blend with floral and smoky notes. This bold, aromatic rum has made waves not just across the province and Canada, but internationally, with availability reaching as far as the UK.

The Newfoundland Distillery's rums reflect the rugged beauty of the Rock itself—complex, full of character, and unmistakably local.

## Chaga Rum

Crafted by The Newfoundland Distillery Co., this rum blends 5-year-old Demerara rum with local chaga mushroom and wild honey. Earthy and sweet, it's a rum that tastes like the island's wilderness in a glass.

*Gold and Silver medals at the New York International Spirit Competition*

*Best Spiced Rum in Canada for Chaga Rum from the World Rum Awards in 2019.*

## Gunpowder and Rose Rum

Also from The Newfoundland Distillery Co., this is aged Jamaican rum infused in Clarke's Beach with wild Newfoundland roses, charred birch, kelp, and sea salt for bold, gunpowder-inspired flavour. It's rugged, floral, and unlike any rum in the world.

*Best Spiced Rum in Canada for Gunpowder and Rose Rum from the World Rum Awards in 2020.*

*Gunpowder and Rose Rum won a silver medal at the 2021 Rum Masters Competition.*

## Maple Rum

This wonderful Maple Rum is made with a deep rich Demerara Rum that is then barrel aged in Clarke's Beach, with maple syrup from Quebec to produce a delicately balanced, perfectly flavoured Maple Rum. Perfect for sipping on, over ice and in all of your favourite rum based cocktails.

# Part V

# Bonus Bar

# Top Rums to Try Before You Die

From rare overproofed bottles to elegant aged classics, here are some rums every true Rummelier must taste in their lifetime.

## Foursquare 2007 (Barbados)

**Why it's special:** A masterclass in traditional rum-making. No sugar, no additives — just oak-aged brilliance from Richard Seale.

**Flavour:** Rich oak, spice, and dried fruit with a dry finish.

## El Dorado 21-Year-Old (Guyana)

**Why it's special:** Distilled in wooden stills you won't find anywhere else on Earth.

**Flavour:** Deep molasses, spice, coffee, and a warm, luxurious finish.

## Hampden Estate Overproof (Jamaica)

**Why it's special:** This is funk in a bottle — pure Jamaican hogo from wild fermentation and pot stills.

**Flavour:** Pineapple, nail polish (yes), tropical fruit, banana, and spice.

## Mount Gay 1703 Master Select (Barbados)

**Why it's special:** Mount Gay is the oldest rum distillery in the world (since 1703), and this is their crown jewel.

**Flavour:** Nutmeg, toffee, toasted oak, and refined vanilla.

## Rhum J.M XO (Martinique – French Agricole Rum)

**Why it's special:** Made from fresh sugarcane juice, not molasses — a completely different rum experience.

**Flavour:** Earthy, grassy, spiced wood, with a dry herbal twist.

## Santa Teresa 1796 (Venezuela)

**Why it's special:** Solera aging gives this rum smoothness that rivals cognac.

**Flavour:** Honey, raisin, tobacco, cinnamon, and silky texture.

## Diplomatico Reserva Exclusiva (Venezuela)

**Why it's special:** A gateway rum — perfect for new enthusiasts who want something rich and sweet.

**Flavour:** Toffee, chocolate, orange peel, and brown sugar.

## Appleton Estate 21-Year-Old (Jamaica)

**Why it's special:** This is the queen of Jamaican elegance, crafted by legendary master blender Joy Spence.

**Flavour:** Orange zest, warm spice, cocoa, and dried fruit.

## Ron Diplomático Single Vintage 2005 (Venezuela)

**Why it's special:** Aged in bourbon and sherry casks — it's dessert in a glass.

**Flavour:** Raisins, creamy vanilla, espresso, and sherry sweetness.

## The Real McCoy 12 Year (Barbados)

**Why it's special:** Authentic, no-added-sugar rum that honors Prohibition legend Bill McCoy.

**Flavour:** Balanced, toasty oak, cinnamon, light molasses.

## Plantation XO 20th Anniversary (Barbados)

**Why it's special:** A beautiful blend of Barbados rums aged in bourbon barrels, then finished in French cognac casks. It's one of the smoothest sippers out there — elegant, tropical, and refined. This special release marks Alexandre Gabriel's 20 years as master blender at Maison Ferrand. It's a Barbados blend of rums aged 8–15 years in ex-bourbon barrels, then taken to France for an additional 2–10 years maturation in small French oak cognac casks.

**Flavour:** Toasted coconut, banana, vanilla, and a lingering note of nutmeg and oak.

**Appearance:** A deep golden-bronze hue, radiating warm cherry-wood tones

## Bonus: Screech (Newfoundland, Canada)

**Why it's special:** Not for complexity — but for culture. You haven't lived till you've been screeched in! Screech is the number-one selling dark rum in Newfoundland and a true cultural icon of the island. Screech being its flagship brand. Known for its bold flavour and rich heritage, it's more than just a drink—it's a rite of passage, often shared during the legendary "Screech-In" ceremonies. If you're visiting Newfoundland, trying Screech isn't just recommended—it's practically mandatory

**Flavour:** Strong, rum-forward, with a history as rich as its taste.

# My Personal Collection & Rare Finds

## The Tasting Table – Centre Stage in the Rum Room

This is where stories are told, legends are tasted, and sometimes—if you're lucky—memories are made. The tasting table in my rum room sits in the heart of hundreds of bottles collected from around the world. Every shelf holds history—from Cuban classics to Filipino favorites, from Barbadian treasures to Dominican secrets. But it's around this round wooden table that the real magic happens. This is where the book came to life, I love talking about rum, the history, the flavours and 600 bottles later!

Friends come, glasses clink, and soon we're solving the world's problems—one rum at a time. Some call it a man cave. I call it my Ministry of Rum Appreciation and General Nonsense.

## Personal Collection

## Pusser's Rum, based on the Royal Navy's original recipe.

## Right Side: Okra Rum Ceramic Sailor Bottles (Trinidad and Tobago)

✦ These are historic Captain Seven Sailor Bottles, a beloved part of Trinidadian rum heritage.

✦ Highly collectible, they depict Caribbean men in sailor uniforms.

✦ The brand is famous for sweet, rich navy-style rum and stunning bottle design.

## Left side: Trinidad Drummer Bottles – Rum, Rhythm and Representation

### Origin and Style:

✦ These bottles are believed to be produced in the 1950s to 1970s, likely handcrafted and painted ceramic or glass.

✦ Modeled after Trinidadian Carnival characters or Shango/Baptist drummers, dressed in vibrant traditional garb.

✦ They were filled with Caribbean rum, often sold to tourists or offered as special limited-edition bottles by local distillers.

### Cultural Significance:

✦ The design reflects the Afro-Caribbean roots of Trinidad, especially in the music, dance, and religious practices like Orisha (Shango) and Carnival masquerade traditions.

✦ Drums are central to these traditions—not just as instruments but as tools of resistance, celebration, and communication.

## Collector's Value:

+ These are now highly collectible, especially when intact and with their original stoppers (like the yellow hat or cap).

+ They're part of a larger series of character bottles that include sailors, dancers, and musicians—each representing a facet of Trinidadian identity and rum's role in storytelling.

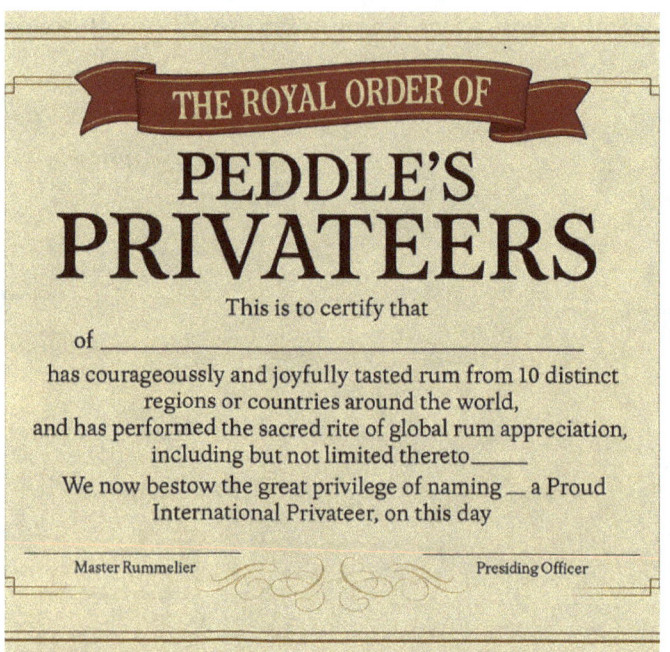

## Jeff Peddle, Master Rummelier®, Canada

This certificate is presented to individuals who have embarked on a spirited journey through the world of rum — sampling from 10 different distilleries or regions across the globe. Each pour tells a tale: of pirates and plantations, of rebellion and revival, of sugarcane, stills, and sea spray.

The final rite is completed at the tasting table in Jeff's Rum Room, where the stories come alive — from the smoky coasts of Islay to the lush valleys of Jamaica, the cask-aged traditions of Barbados, to the sweet overproof legends of Newfoundland.

Only those who sip with curiosity, listen with respect, and toast with joy are welcomed into this honorary rank. The Royal Order of Peddle's Privateers celebrates not just rum — but heritage, humour, and a love of exploration.

> Raise your glass and wear the title proudly — you've earned it.

# Rum and Food Pairings

## Cakes, Skewers and Cocktails

## Newfoundland Rum Cake (Nan's "Now We're Talkin'" Cake)

This version uses molasses, dark Newfoundland rum, and warm spices. Perfect for winter nights, family gatherings, or when you're snowed in with no chance of going anywhere.

Ingredients:

For the Cake:

- 1 cup brown sugar
- ½ cup molasses
- ½ cup butter (room temp)
- 2 eggs
- 1½ cups flour
- 1 tsp baking soda
- 1 tsp cinnamon
- ½ tsp nutmeg
- ¼ tsp allspice
- ½ tsp salt
- ½ cup buttermilk
- ½ cup dark Newfoundland rum (like Screech or Old Sam)
- 1 cup raisins or mixed dried fruit (soaked in rum overnight if you're serious)
- Optional: ½ cup chopped walnuts or pecans

For the Rum Sauce (a must-have):

- ½ cup butter
- 1 cup brown sugar
- ¼ cup water
- ¼ cup dark rum (plus a little extra "for the chef")

Instructions:

1. Preheat oven to 325°F. Grease and flour a bundt or loaf pan.
2. Cream together the butter, brown sugar, and molasses.
3. Add eggs one at a time, beating after each.
4. In a separate bowl, mix flour, baking soda, salt, and spices.
5. Slowly add dry mixture to the wet, alternating with buttermilk.
6. Stir in rum, soaked raisins (drained), and nuts if using.
7. Pour into pan and bake for 55–65 minutes, or until a toothpick comes out clean.
8. While the cake bakes, make the rum sauce: combine butter, brown sugar, and water in a saucepan. Bring to a boil, reduce heat and simmer 3–4 mins. Remove from heat, stir in rum.
9. Once the cake is done, poke holes all over it while warm and pour half the sauce overtop.
10. Let sit for 20 minutes, then remove from pan and drizzle with remaining sauce.

Bonus Tip:

Wrap leftovers (if there are any!) in parchment and foil—it gets even better after a day or two

"This ain't your average cake—it's how Newfoundlanders celebrate, mourn, apologize, and say I love you… all in one slice."

# Classic Caribbean Rum Cake
# (aka "Get-Tipsy Cake")

Ingredients:

- 1 box yellow cake mix
- 1 box (3.4 oz) instant vanilla pudding
- 4 eggs
- ½ cup vegetable oil
- ½ cup water
- ½ cup dark rum (Jamaican or spiced preferred)
- ½ cup chopped pecans (optional)

Rum Glaze:

- ½ cup butter
- ¼ cup water
- 1 cup sugar
- ½ cup dark rum

Instructions:

1. Preheat oven to 325°F. Grease and flour a Bundt pan.
2. Sprinkle nuts in the bottom if using.
3. Mix cake mix, pudding, eggs, oil, water, and rum. Pour into pan.
4. Bake 50–60 minutes or until a toothpick comes out clean.
5. While baking, make glaze: melt butter, stir in water and sugar, bring to boil. Remove from heat and stir in rum.
6. When cake is done, poke holes in the top and slowly pour glaze over it. Let soak before removing from pan.

Rum Tip: Let it sit overnight. The longer it rests, the boozier the bite.

# Rum-Glazed Jerk Shrimp Skewers

Ingredients:

- 1 lb large shrimp, peeled and deveined
- 2 tbsp olive oil
- 2 tbsp jerk seasoning
- 1 tbsp lime juice

Rum Glaze:

- ¼ cup dark rum
- 2 tbsp brown sugar
- 1 tbsp honey
- 1 tsp soy sauce
- 1 tsp grated ginger
- Pinch of chili flakes (optional)

Instructions:

1. Toss shrimp with olive oil, jerk seasoning, and lime juice. Marinate 30 mins.
2. Thread shrimp onto skewers.
3. In a small saucepan, combine glaze ingredients and simmer until slightly thickened.
4. Grill shrimp skewers 2–3 mins per side, brushing with glaze during last minute.
5. Serve hot with extra glaze on the side.

# Rum Punch – Island Style

Ingredients:

- 1 part lime juice
- 2 parts simple syrup
- 3 parts dark or overproof rum
- 4 parts fruit juice (pineapple, orange, or guava work great)
- Dash of Angostura bitters
- Grated nutmeg (optional)
- Ice and fruit slices to garnish

Instructions:

1. Mix all ingredients in a large pitcher with ice.
2. Stir well and taste test (careful—it sneaks up on you).
3. Serve chilled in glasses garnished with fruit or a paper umbrella if you're feeling fancy.

# Rum Goodwill

As part of my undying love for rum—and with the generous support of a few rum-loving partners in crime—I donated a full-blown Rum Tree to the Festival of Trees in Fort McMurray for the Northern Lights Health Foundation. Valued at $8,000, it had more bottles than a St. John's wedding and got more attention than Santa himself. Let's just say… it was the only tree in the room that could cause a hangover.

> "One part sour, two parts sweet, three parts strong, four parts weak… and a dash of regret if you have too many."

# Sources & Acknowledgments

No book worth reading writes itself—and this one is no different. The stories, history, and humour in these pages were inspired by real people, long voyages (some mine, some not), and more than a few great rums shared along the way. Most of my sources stem from the adventures I have had through Barbados, Martinique, Dominican Republic, Jamaica, India, and beyond.

A heartfelt thank you to CBC News for their article "Remembering Wince Worthman — the man who brought Lamb's to Newfoundland," published March 11, 2018. Much of what I wrote about Wince came from this piece—and the rest came from personal memories. I was lucky enough to do business with him over the years and even luckier to share a drink of Lamb's with him. He was one of a kind.

I also want to thank the Master Rummelier Group. Their community helped take my knowledge of rum to the next level. Greg Hill and Matt Pietrek, in particular, deserve special mention. Their teachings, insights, and books gave me a deeper appreciation of the global rum scene—and a clearer sense of what makes a great rum truly great.

Many of the facts and stories in this book came from reading and researching online, digging through public archives, and sometimes just falling down the rabbit hole of rum history on a late night. From 18th-century naval records to the story of how NASCAR was fueled by rumrunners, every twist was worth the ride.

But most of all, this book was shaped by travel. I've been blessed to visit distilleries around the world—Barbados, Jamaica, Dominican Republic, St. Martin, and beyond—where I talked with rum makers, walked through aging rooms, and tasted liquid gold straight from the barrel. Each experience added a story, a lesson, or a laugh.

To everyone who ever poured a glass, shot a tail, or simply pointed me toward a good bottle—thank you.

To the Vardy's, Long's, Walsh's, and all the great friends along the way—this book's for you. Cheers to the stories, the laughter, and the rum that brought us together.

And may your liver be as strong as your opinions after three drinks.

If not, at least make sure someone else paid for the bottle.

And to my sister Donna, who drank holy water while we drank rum—bless her heart, she keeps praying daily for all of us boys.

This book is as much yours as it is mine.

# Final Toast – "May Yer Big Jib Always Draw"

To all who joined me on this rum-soaked journey—cheers to you.

May your glass never be empty, your stories always be colourful, and your friends just wild enough to make you nervous.

And as we say back home: May your big jib always draw.

(If you're not from Newfoundland… look it up. Then pour yourself a drink and raise a glass to the Rock.)

Thanks for taking the time to read Rum 101 for Dummies Like Me. I'm just a small independent writer with a big love for rum, stories, and the places I've been lucky enough to visit. If you enjoyed the book, give me a shout on Facebook and let me know what you loved—or what made you laugh. Your kind words (and your rum recommendations) mean the world.

Jeff Peddle

## About the Author

Jeff Peddle was born in Labrador City, raised in Newfoundland, and spent years working on George Street—earning a reputation as the guy who could break up a bar fight and pour a shot of Lamb's in the same breath. A world traveller, master Rummelier, and storyteller by blood, Jeff's adventures have taken him from tiki bars to pirate hideouts, with more laughs than a Legion meat draw. He's the kind of guy who shows up with a rum bottle in one hand, a tale in the other, and always leaves folks smiling.

www.ingramcontent.com/pod-product-compliance
Lightning Source LLC
Chambersburg PA
CBHW070051120426
42742CB00048B/2043